Waking from Myself

OTHER BOOKS OF PREVERBS

Verbal Paradise (preverbs) (Zasterle Press, 2011)

Glossodelia Attract (preverbs) (Station Hill Press, 2015)

Things Done for Themselves (preverbs) (Marsh Hawk Press, 2015)

The Daimon of the Moment (preverbs) (Talisman House Press, 2015)

Not Even Rabbits Go Down This Hole (preverbs) (Spuyten Duyvil, 2020)

Black Scintillation (preverbs) (Lunar Chandelier Collective Press, 2021)

Waking From Myself (preverbs) (Station Hill Press, 2022)

ONLINE SERIES OF PREVERBS WITH PHOTOS BY SUSAN QUASHA

Genius Foci
talismanmag.net

Hilaritas Sublime
metambesen.org

Hearing Other
dispatchespoetrywars.com

Dowsing Axis
dispatchespoetrywars.com

Surface Retention
metambesen.org

View of the Sleeping Dragon
blazingstadium.com

Waking from Myself

preverbs

George Quasha

Station Hill Press

BARRYTOWN

Copyright © 2022 George Quasha

All rights reserved. Except for short passages for purposes of review, no part of this book may be reproduced in any form or by any means, electronic or mechanical, including photocopying, recording, or by any information storage and retrieval system, without permission in writing from the publisher.

Published by Station Hill Press, the publishing project of the Institute for Publishing Arts, Inc., 120 Station Hill Road, Barrytown, NY 12507, New York, a not-for-profit, tax-exempt organization [501(c)(3)].

Online catalogue: www.stationhill.org
e-mail: publishers@stationhill.org

Design: Susan Quasha
Front cover art: Axial Drawing, acrylic paint on paper, by George Quasha
Back cover photo of author, 2018, by Susan Quasha
Axial Drawing (graphite), c. 2008, by George Quasha, on part title pages

Library of Congress Cataloging-in-Publication Data

Names: Quasha, George, author.
Title: Waking from myself : preverbs / George Quasha.
Description: Barrytown, NY : Station Hill Press, [2021]
Identifiers: LCCN 2021045430 | ISBN 9781581772074 (paperback)
Subjects: LCGFT: Poetry.
Classification: LCC PS3567.U28 W35 2021 | DDC 811/.54—dc23
LC record available at https://lccn.loc.gov/2021045430

Printed in the United States of America

beyond right

reading

for Susan Quasha

Contents

tuning by fire

for Burt Kimmelman

work is its own surrender

Now that you're here, come in. It's talking.
Thank you for coming to help sustain the unsustainable.
Together is the further of letting go.
The poem takes the guesswork out of knowing who I am and implants uncertainty.

It's positively a poem never asking the status of saying until it's too late.
Eternal truths sugarcoated are changing their tune behind our backs.
The middle ages are still in crisis.

Faust has us ever further.
The late name breaking memories is mantra no devil hears.
No music lulls us here.

I write nightly so the work can lose itself with no concern for my attachment.
Inspiration empties the work of our need for it, frees it of myself.
I know the line is coming when the hand is leaving me behind.

The poem is where the poet envisions a possible reader.
That you can't find yourself here is a sign of hope.
A free space is where no image is safe.

As death never lets us off the hook self-true art imitates death.
Poetry excavates knowing gone silent.
Eyes go both ways.

Ego flays what stays.
Poem talks as if tongue strikes flint.
Fire in the hole has untold toll.

2 *a buddha keeps the truth about self to herself*

I let the mirror break to get me further in.
The moment comes to embrace the dark spot even leopards won't wear.
It's the further life of *no* that keeps me going.

People secretly seek confirmation and comfort in art at their peril.
In the matrix of mystery ecstasy stalks death beyond all understanding.
Artist creates viewer over his dead body.

It's perilous keeping the view of peril perilous.
No point wishing I haven't said these things because I haven't.
Rise again if for no other reason to prove you can.

Art for being's sake is a dark alley seeing with owl eyes rarely promotes.
Truth laid bare flays aware.
No place to camp.

I forget what "I" have written but this hand remembers better.
Poetics shelters smart cover-up of frustrating intelligence.
The guard is in the door, ajar here, so you appear.

Apparent randomness spurs attention to loosen lids in drift to atemporal tenor.
A line is an act of remembering what is not yet before.
The words wield in tongues across the page trippingly.

What happened is what's happening.
The punch line is beyond redemption.
The effort to reason through is doomed necessity.

3 *coherent non understanding*

Absence of attitudes makes crazy.
No hiding behind knowing or not what you're saying.
I hear a speaking bounding about the clairauditorium in search of a mouth.

Mind feedbacks off the head hit wall.
Time to re-anatomize inquiry.
Certainties need not apply.

Trust the hand that turns the page to know what to say.
Language knows that things happening one after another are not continuous.
Assembling is what words do when left to their own advices.

We think short-lived stamped large ongoing with forever mind.
Between everything is sudden.
Focus in there is spreading legs when not playing dead.

Duende is thriving at the limen of dying.
Teetering to rise with fearful bright eyes.
The dead speak when the asking is right.

Language unlearns.
Subsyntactics convey the unstoried lying under told.
No time holds true.

My life rolls out not knowing how long the roll.
Continuity stitches the going lusional cosmos ever in play.

Exiting a work makes room as never before.

I'm calling obsessed with literal glossolabial spaces open in the fact of saying so.
Rhythm is kept beforehand and then it starts like now. Now.
A poem can begin by ending from the start, ghosting at the periphery of thought.

It's not fully on the page but pushing up between physical elements of focus.

The meaning is stored in the reading.
Where it's coming from follows where it's going.
How I know is how I hear.

I'm not even sure now is happening but that otherwise what.
A verbal element is a hot rock in the hand holding up.
The status of the statement is just out of reach.

I find unaccountable the fact finding.
The mind circles its wagons in vain.
It sure has a lot of sure things to be sure about while never forgetting it.

It offers a score with premonitory transparency.
See through is the kind of seeing inevitable in the music, audible as we speak.
Clear pressure pressures clearly.

Earth offers a clear sign everything can surface.
Seeing evolves according to who's saying.
Avoid interfering with your own incursions.

Let's say we're traveling on this surface coming to seem as mind itself seems.
Seemingly priority is an aptitude of the apt seer.

We've been here forever and we're just passing through.
Why talk as though already dead but that the dead talk when talk's not dead.
Textual transparency reveals that it is an acquired taste with one taste.

Roughshod is an attribute of a difficult verbal birth right there in front of you. Ride.
No doubt I was dreaming when I said I heard your mind getting tangled preverbial.
Self-commentary is unnecessary so it is possible.

Over time the real poem in undertime comes up behind in mind.
Look it in the eyes and it turns its head away.
The world can be born everyday because it is abandoned.

The memorable is behind us.
The poem is not taking it lying down.

Open all your eyes when it looks into you.
You are the stranger between than which none more than you.

At dawn the night is still talking, down to a murmur.
My only defense is I'm listening and I know it's there but not the way thought.

Death is substantially here already, just under the threshold of tolerance.
It's touchable in your personal timelessness.
You know its moment as a devil cannot find it.

Speaking of ashes vs. speaking in ashes.
Hovering at the edge of sleep you may be ruled by two worlds at once.
Learning to speak the between is not the bier.

There's a moment in the dance when the eyes see through.
Here is where you see them seethrough.
The sacrifice begins with any identity at all.

Giving up hope is not hopeless.
Tens of thousands breathe away death together, it's one of those moments.

Verbal revirgination is not getting unfucked.
Saying still gores.
The open air threatens dark dance giving future.

At any moment your mind runs scale invariant along the median.
Dead center homing in is incandescing until bounding.

No pun intends it but things do fuse to say the more they are.
Every engagement with the daimon is an homage to itself in home flow.
Things happen two ways at once and one way at twice, same time, same place, new.

We've been detained by ambiguity.
There's undertow in undertime.
Eternity is a dimension of song after song.

Still kicking time around to know I'm here.
Poem is talking for itself while I'm giving up.
Knowing so suddenly you don't know it's knowing.

The pronouns startle thinking for themselves.
I'm lost and now I'm found thought after thought in no time round.

Every morning runs against a grain.
Every meaning is sudden.

The hand knows before the head.
We're working up to the inside track.

Speaking under pressure language moves toward speaking for itself.
Gut listening moves along an inaudible edge.

Samsara is the play in the gears, the line, aligning living here—sounds out.
From one end to another pulling to push the meanings into their scatterback.

Preparing mood to meet life square disprepares in lifelike why. Why me?
Better not eat it all up.

Staying too much indigests.
The tracks lead back into themselves.

Listening cross culture shocks the same into crossover dimensions.
Look for me in undertime, new reads facing out.

The real poetry is always to read, yet to read—never to have read.
The matrix is unborn at the lift of a pen.

A devil owns no pen but your own.
Duende implies co-haunting.
Insider inflammation gives rise.

If I were any kind of poet I'd slide down the pole in a hole of the whole saying this.
Off-center recursion invites the jump by uninvited incursion.

I feel born off.
Existing takes torque.

I repent my imperfect reception of the world wild at large, but it's not helping.
If only we'd known there's fire in the hole.

Things only mean what they mean where they mean.
Who knows what knows when it knows.
Each thing flavors away.

It's how you move about on the surface that finds the beloved.
Syntax flex sexes.
You can't even say it happens with a straight face, or not.

Supra segmentation inflection flays what it says for you.
Not all tunes straighten.
Her mouth shapes out heartfelt etym in high fly, onliving.

The sentence forgets how it began by the time it gets here.
Poetry is just like us.
Only bigger in how it seems behind everything. Imagine the verb.

The verb is however you make it go. Let go.
The surface unmoves in the unmoving eye.
That the fire rage wherefore forgetting is not.

Watch what you say, the book is listening.
Sudden speaking is speaking waking now.

Every true message is your last message to the world.
The line stays open to stay fresh life first.
It sees birth backwards for starters.

There's barely enough time to live, except right now.

A sentence is moving forgetfully with faithful direction.
The beginning is in the end never knowing itself the first time let alone the last.
Poetry is language committed to learning itself.

The book's a site of back readability—unimpressive yet pressing in.
Compression slips in a verbal depth of field.
Any word hums in a manner of mouthing *full.*

The poem is new when you can say this is not poetry.
It's all in how we do denial.
All the same the line arrives just in time to dawn. Birds!

Like the minimum it hums with rime and reason.
If it sounds real it bounds real.
Poetry is thinking sensorial.

A thing said true eternalizes in a flash.
The unknown is talking back as we speak.
Mind on the ground, feet down the page.

10 *liliacladelia*[1]

Don't talk to me about themes and keep your memes to yourself, spoken oneiric.
What matters is the tongue is your own if you're going to speak in it.

There's passion in syllables at play, just not whose you'd think.
They have feelings, only in tones with timing.

A sign so to speak is looking for a post.
Take *paradosis* as in handing down *the message*—fact or fiction or another dream?

I'm late I'm late for an unimportant fact of date.
Time floats as you float and contrariwise.

The title here is a dream word: that's a fact.
It's staring you in the face is a mood of the text in hand passing on what it is.

Gods don't incarnate to please follows from a mood of poetic grammar.
It rises to mind on a trinitarian something. It's timing.

A life is on a trajectory and it's porous.
If the poetic line gets inside the course it resets.

Life the person living interiorizes the poem trajecting.
Read me inside what must be hearing it on.

A poem has an outside we see from in here against the sky.
It refloats you as you face up hands open timely.

---

1 Future word predicted in dream, meaning delayed.

seed reading

A dream word implies a dream world like a living language, lived so.
Just laying eyes on certain books shifts dimension, think preverbial rug pulled out.

There's a grammar tracking false endings.
It feels falling off in the failing verb.

Anything possible to be read in the line is a sliver of the truth.
A splinter in the failing truth says why we cry.

The standard of necessity in saying just this much may hide as a safety precaution.
The body of language receives you bodily.

Reading seeds. *Seed has no contrary.*
In text time flower back to the present caught up between words, thorns.

Horns in the flesh of torero which to say tears through time.
Duende plumbs gravity in tongue.

In the dream trial she calls herself whore with scarlet pride having her *her* way.
O lente lente currite noctis equi dreaming her way in the line, ovarian, Ovidian.
I hear forever in her.

It's the holes in the middle that matter.
In the dream I'm trying to explain this to two friends—she lifts off mind her way.
Action is absolute in its dimension.

The poem does not tell all for my own good.
Language escapes religion as catch can.

If I were looking for a way out you'd have given it to me long ago, so hanging am I.
Anything said in person surprises here among the falling stones.
Always on trial by self prosecution.

A word is a turn on the focus wheel.
New objects from old make bold my inner fool.
Root pro*jects*. What verbs verb from the thing. Action in and out of view.

A grammar of false endings precedes speaking having been.
There, there, the gut rush bespeaking spoken truly.
O life of strife strip back down.

Saying rescues at the level of call down.
If you don't know there's a vision how can you know the vision's happening?
Thinking knowing what is said is making a lot of noise.

Gorgeous noise is recourse in full stream.
My thinking was printed in my walking walking her way.
The mind is its own place/and in itself can make…

Her body reality is asking to be asked.
One sarod is not one save as oneself, is saying it's not one, goes without saying.
No wonder it wonders with wonder.

Killing egos makes more egos, mirrors with a vengeance.
Words disappear in your ear but you know they're there.
I disjoin in the hot place.

13

Milking the unknown is still home.
What matters is gesture integrates.
Failure stalks in every word.

A hurdle is the whirl of mind from behind.
Non-coercive disruption celebrates.
The line is a lifeline in a room so small no one fits.

A world tires until it fires.

The way things mean keeps changing its mind.
Am I missing something in what's not up to me?

Poem is forging a reader in the gut.
Is it a boy? Is it a girl? Or a golem mirroring a mind it finds?
A tall tale is telling in series its nano-novels.

Other writing loved is my other possible self saying what I can't.
I'm making a bed for as yet undeclared enemies of seeing through.
Gulls on Tuckernuck Island are talking more than I dare, all in a day's say.

It's this pen scratching your echo on its way home.
Contrarily there's everything to say since nothing has been said to stay.
Study your leaking pen.

A poem gives the thing its say otherwise silenced.
The Visionary Chariot is a name like mind streaking with Rainbow Body.
Enterprise in walking naked gives out in a world unmirroring.

14 *staying tuned hot*

...the common risks of language where
failure stalks in every word...
Lord Byron

Everything is what it is when it happens should be obvious but never is.
It's not reality if it's not showing its underskirting intemperate flood matrix.

Time tricks as it travels.
Addiction to tracking travails.

I can bathe in my own texts in that they are definingly not mine like water.
Like all waters there's no likeness in flow.

I'd say this is beyond use but use is self-evident beyond this need to say.
Text weaves like liquid crystal, remembering in the flow slowing.

A poem is an absolute with relative impact and self true subtract.
Life's distraction from death includes waiting for the other shoe to drop.

Do I repeat myself, but then repeating does not do.
Taking seriously is taking your sense of humor more than seriously.

On the other hand there's firsthand.
Blake sees you back.

This incursion is not looking like track marks.
Me as me means not much.
The me it speaks to is willing to reinvent a reader in myself, seeing me back.

It's unexpected. All the better for the worse for wear still to bear.
Life is still talking down to me with recognition, checking back seeing.

What's the singer saying so sunken in tormenting sound, she asks.
It quests in its question, ragged.
The song serpent frowns to tune in darkly.

Having said so tells a story that digs in deeper soon available for plucking.
Falling in love stone first on the fly.
Soul search turbulence stretches sinews.

It's about getting inside to stay.

Line to line is meant to be as good as saying life to life.
The language is artificial enough to carry the strange charge over to heart line.
Therefore this is spoken like a… like a…

If it fits the mouth in the actual turn, swung by lip, talk tip of the wave, say so.
You hear it every time at the one time.
Insider hearing breaks the rules and levels.

Staying inside includes jumping stories while still elevating and down again.
It has a tune and a flip side.
Gypsy transmissions in the Pataphysical blood flood with torque.

The two together is a ratchet with sublingual reverse.
It's what has to get said in the history of the world, whirled.
Someone has to hear the cry twist out still wisely held in or history is not really.

Listening is the historian with stirring feet talking.
There's a big earth mouth that never stops calling out calling it song in song.

I would track who's tracking to find out where I am when not here.
The start is knowing I have nothing to say being myself here to be said.
There's a certain distraction that lets me go on without knowing how.

Not repetition but relevance counts on. And on.
Finding out how to be there when it happens and no know how.
Nano tunes tone nature timely.

Declaration matricizes midsentence.
The event preserves and opens out back the heart of the matter implanting.
The singer declares lineage in every name.

No one can say you can't.
No one can lie with a straight face but laughs that the mirror image flood.
The poem emerges with the condition that nothing stops even when it stops.

An ecstatic moment image of eternity's telling as the frog's eye tells the frog's brain.
At swim the image.
Field speaks as all along and anywhere at once.

Remembering all words verb itself verbs aural.

Surrendering in line loosens the links letting words become their other.
Multi-storied fielding sense zones offer sanguinated loding in course.
Swift ears listen slower.

Think guitar miming the nature of mind in its mode of non-operation.
Large spaces compose when heard.

The body writes itself out with handy obedience.
Anything at all is a wake-up call.

The poem is a seeming series like life falling forward.
A waking line self re-regulates en route.
Unremembering who I am dements consciously.

The inner demagogue gets his fidgety fingers in the phonic flaps without notice.
Ignorance is that misses the force to over read or under relieve.
Now, now cannot be said enough.

Zero point refreshes.

All the degrees of intention bound with sliding sides.
Sensing thinks that thinking senses.

A disciple of intended losing out I have to ask: Am I up to it?
A thinking shadows me wherever I go.
You have to taste it in the dark to know it.

With that feeding you cease knowing you're feeding.
The thinking is the part you can't look to.
The grip is that the story is at large.

Memory edits according to angular emphasis.
Vocal body edits down to cell demagoguery to spring the higher leak.

No tricks you must say at the entrée.

Language means everything it says.
This is no time to cut back.
Even here back seems very distant. Even scoping.

Soul economies spread with missing links.
This said even now is getting away.
Fortunately we are not being thrown all the way out.

Who can give up feeling too much from top to bottom.

Talking triggers an interaction with the reality of sacrifice.
Deer in my ear?
Intrinsically intelligently speaking the work is out of its bottle.

Possible music is what is needed to hear.
Despair precedes calling up.
The dream impedes saying what it is.

The missing between never ceases emptying in unthoughts, some danceable.
No time is like absence.
Knowing this feels a lot more than it's willing to say.

Dream comprises my chest pressed against a membrane heart of everything that is.
Middle voice: Presenting a chance to know everything at once in anything at all.
To be safe let's just say and vice versa.

The language speaks but without bottom minus my own.
You disbelieve it can be true to not know so vividly.

19 *feral peril*

Reading's believing.
I admit to studying studying saying so.
And I reject help until dire desire.

Secretly reading turns inside out.
Falling backwards orienting is being caught already in trusted arms.
Now I'm believing in eternity beyond belief.

Catch me again, out, more out.
There are no either/or's this far in, along.
The between time is a gap if you're getting the god's eye view.

Received means you didn't quite do it.
It has to not be seen coming.
The waver in the mind is the wave rising unseen. Then there's flutter.

Otherwise *I*'m in waiting, pronominally intensified and freely reclaimed.
Further free the fantasy of the other's hearing.
Longing goes feral and further.

Reading goes all the way into the dark heart of the forest.
See Spot flip.
We know it's a listening field wherefore it instructs in itself.

A performative middle voice promise I do here and now.
To be true. To my own. Unselfconsciousness.

It takes a turn for the force. [*feel the lingual backwash*]

You see me here in this partial body not fully represented.
The genius is out of the rattle.

A line is a line in the sand to straddle.
A language hides its secrets in the sayable.

Receiving is not an act of will.
Each thing its eternity unbelieved.

A line stakes a site to reorient in the round, figuratively speaking.
Any language has its secrets unbeknownst, still groaning.

There is no escaping working the self image.
Nothing is completed so long as we are observing.

On even days I know more than I give myself credit for.
On odd days I'm not as smart as I think I am. *This is a hyper-selfie.*

If a god poked a finger through the page the poem guarantees you wouldn't notice.
You'd accept safe passage and move on.

Sin detection is the wrong kind of vigilance.
There is no being forewarned.

I'm feeling realer now said forth.
Ragged ragas rescue.

It quickens to flesh out.

21 *arbitrating vehicular identity*

Some questions are like kites in the night sky.
How many the ways of untrue figuring? For example.
Truly speak untrue.

The time between lines grows in gardening.
Feel free to lead a double life, you do anyway.
Language controls from the inside and no looking.

The gesture says you're here.
You can't ride out the text the devil fails to find.
Its womanly unity is dancing solo naturally and not, by rights.

It's only dance if it exhausts body and soul in situ.
You don't know it coming into you with no opposition. Uncontrariwise.
Hellfire bright between tongues strikes up the wand in the wag.

It's a poem courting religious envy.
The daimon knows your mind over its edge rarely happy happily.
Teaching is ownness in free fall even more happily.

Happy to be here seeing you're here at long last longingly.
Joy in numbers subs for possible selves in free fly.
It's music if bleeding is painless.

Poetry longs religiously binding in sheer breathing vow tooth and claw.
A word pulls meaning out from under itself until it lights up, striking.
Person scarcely survives being in her body saying so and yet to come.

Stepping up intensity finds the ordinary otherwise.
Finding wanting is along the way.

Without warning I become what I want to be as I am.
The kicking sound says let Faust out of your heart.

Enlightenment is only between lines and further between betweens.
Suddenly the space inside the things there broke loose inside me.

And I said look inside where only outside stares back.
Everything is standing out from itself waiting for the call to see in.

The morning practices slowly through the body.
A poetic act is framework of rebalancing disparate energies ready to talk at last.

Old bones crack to borrow heat.
Then they talk back.

Ambiguity requests in the open.

The point that Satan cannot find is palpable body center where the day gathers.
A line strings points in momentous momentum to balance between zeros.

Reading poignantly of death I die a little, instructed.
One vase breaking vases break across time hence this cracked light display.

Inconclusion strategizes the free journey.

23

Unbelievable reading is to the root of itself.
Nothing to say on my sarod while it plays on for a part of itself.

Knowing the word means more than you say perturbs until it swirls.
A word breaks off from the word before.
The poem breaks off from the world.

The created reader comes out from behind the mark.
She reported a light illuminating both sides of the equation unevenly.
The light appeared more solid than the objects shown.

The poetics: light or light-up?

Memorially sculpted needs to be incorporated in the view.
Truly untrue benefits of the whole imperfectly.
Hilaritas shows self a self service machine.

To have not been thought before realizes.
Where does the weight fall perplexes the tongue in question.
Apologies in advance for the failing footfall beat.

Micro ragas make up the voice to get physical.
Free to fake fears not being.
A poem offers itself what religion needed to be or die on the vine.

Bodying remolds word worlds.
Now you hear it now you don't.

Now for preverbial propaganda for limited understanding in unconstrained holding.
Every word a matrix of meaning for starters.

I sit still and time unfolds just like that.
Word by word a flash in mystery.

The world falls away all by itself just like me.
It sounds like noise but now I know it's just back talking.

It never repeats but it self justify.
Count the ways it turns on itself.

So hard to believe it goes on forever.
Accepting being alone with itself it says so.

Just sounding out here.
The real deal peal.

It stops short to stand under itself.
Momentous momentum is from this very word to the next.

Stopping short is before too far along.
The continuum is two ways at once or it wouldn't continue.

The framework appeals in surround.
A raga acts its spiritual.

Taking refuge in the hidden swing is a rash bliss.

Now for the inevitable.

Committing fresh is commitment to fresh.
Finding one's way along the inner shell curve learning acts upon the thing there.
It's always like you're just seeing it.

Stake it where you can fit it.
You say the thing beside the thing you wanted to say.
Its object makes you object.

All about the poetic mind's finding itself when there's nowhere to be.
Sub axes spur on.
Emoting acts.

All about focus of attention when it all spreads about wilder.
The poem lies in waking.
No need to renounce things that renounce themselves.

Accordingly life is tracking out its own eternity as we speak.
There's no stopping beating out the vintage.
Working the thing vs. studying it—or the two between.

Feeling pulled in and out at once.
Telling doubles triples.
It matures in tense timing in a state of release.

Tension of time types like a verb.

The thing said so as to be believed sooner or later gospelizes.
A thing said is the thing known said.
Saying it right is asking what in it is it.

Chewing's believing.
A good question is not in search of the truth.
To find meaning anywhere at all oracles all and everything.

Except this. The call of the wild.
The mind does not encompass the poem. Let alone the woods. Words.
In nature congruence is temporary.

Incongruence precedes congruence as nonsense sense. Also following.
If your mind now says *true* it caught on the thought—*happiness!* briefly.
Psyche aims to please without freezing.

Magic dances at more than one wedding at once.
The poem does not encompass the mind.
Telling troubles before it doubles.

One vase-breaking vase breaks across time on the path leading out front.
Magic pieces through the picking and you come out piece by piece.
She comes out saying the thing *beside* the thing you wanted to say.

Don't go thinking the Buddha can't chew gum, need she add.
The singing at the edge is not singing until you hear it through and over.

After song the resonance unto unsong.

In the garden she barely recalls the lifelong disease of forcing knowledge.
Her long dharma's the raw.

The word hides the real until you read.
Parts are infinitely more talkative than the whole that *is* not, silent momentum.

Forgive failed seduction.
We is few.

Everything speaks in accents making more, measured so.
We give the names to wear them through to their other side.

I sought the phrase hanging in the air mindfirst.
Mind mired in trivia makes for big instrument extraction.

We're after a good talking to.
Listening is eventual.

Art voices dying underheard.
Celebrate to keep the option opening.

Dakini is figuring and me not figuring out.
Speaking speaks for itself, kindlier.

Saying-I voice as *I* voices says more than I ever manage.
The genius is out of the bottle says the genie in the throttle.

We've come to the end again for the first time and this place knows it.

If language meant to communicate only it would be bent on simples and simplers.
Evolution draws down but only apparently.

Saying without set-up is a set of its own unknowns knowing.
You could dance it with its own feet.

The activity is that can only exist with you there.

The kilter sways in play, word out of word ordering.
Who be born be torn.

Hearing is homing.
When you hear my voice it's even less mine.

The world holds back until hearing aggresses.
Your mind is the poem's instrument, not its aim.

The poetics of the inside job skips relevance.
Were ice cream manna the craving had sex drive.

Secretly death wants you to celebrate other.
Just so my bio inscribes forebears in our other other, *olé!*

I explain into words exfoliate to see myself beyond the end still syntactic, just.
Language norms at its peril.

No telling it's happening until it has you over and out.

Playing the song as it slips out retreats from the act to let the animal out.
It's hunting down its animation.

Wearing earth intimately mind shows in its fashion.
Finding out is what you don't know about what you know.

Who made that sound is the quest questioning self configuring.
It has no cause to give cause.

I lose my way having something to say.
I delay hearing home.

The word mystifies itself without your mouth to go on.
The image is what you're left with.

First encounter face masks.
An image is desiring for itself as we speak.

It's way of getting personal is by relieving us of personality.
Meet me in my house of endless interior I've never been through.

I'm a puppet to the mask doing the talking.
What lies beneath the surface is the story turning truer on its own.

The mask favors the no one we are behind our scenes.
The play declares yourself a free zone.

Someone has entered the room from a previously unavailable door.

I hear knocking and I assume the unseen.
I turned my head and the day had flipped.
Having words with you in a world of only surface suffices if surfed.

A true line finds god in the tall tales doing a job on you.
It masks ever more the no one we are behind our best scenes.
What you see is what gets you first.

The poem tells you what fits where, for now.
What I call a life is behind the writing fronting for me.
Olympically poetry is a contact sport with a moving front line.

Quite unexpected the earth bespeaks vitalography of things achieved.
What knows what this means given oneself on the line?
Giving meaning a black eye calls tongue to further seeming.

In life we get caught up because we never get caught up.
Fall down go boom doesn't just terminate.
Performative perfective reflexive carries over remainders.

Pride of the peacock declares yourself a free zone for reality remix, *olé!*
Glorious word scrimmage takes no sides.
Perfection in what flexes all through reshapes true.

Owner of the house names what can't be mine by nature.
The stakes are wry.
The image speaks at the first blush of the thing.
Perfect flux is not perfective yet perfectly wakes what it flexes.

31 *reaching demonia seeing itself aflower*

Singularity is the secret name of possibility.
Ontononymous the Particular

Life is touch and go and slow, and then time tells, fast.
Words are beyond words and some know it.
One name one demon, not on my watch.

A preverb cuts to the chase no chaser.
The exogamous poem passes felt fidelities on its way home.
No buddha frog left behind, warts on call.

Disregard things that don't speak, but then there aren't any.
Mind can't stop melding terrifying delights.
Light enhanced demonics empty any set entered.

Words are well beyond words before phoning home.
A true syntax realizes interspecific.
It sources other so other I feel the same, preserved.

I holds this dream of charming snakes together.
It takes time to show up and takes time away.
Half way along you feel it nudging from under and showing your tracks.

I feel the end before I open my mouth and I still never get there.
This boney feeling promises health of a strange kind.
Words fall behind unspoken and get me ahead of myself—danger!

Dream fears for me like a mirror for its cracks.
It feeds back in charms.
It has arms, must be mine.

I never knew I was a dancer until I drew sentient curves.
The meaning comes in flashes like strumming paper.

Play on words mirrors words' play in us.
Thinking matters as if souls incarnate streaming.

When you can't imagine a bounding burst you're at the breathing edge.

I'm writing myself notes I know I'll never read—keepsakes too keep me safe.
I don't understand moods which reminds me I don't understand language.
That there is safety in not doing swims in two streams.

What mistakes in a living pool?

A word is well before ill.
Who doesn't love a good bad mood.
O perverse imp my semblable source, speak while my mouth is open.

Two musics bleed two-ways at once.
Three makes two more lives at once where no one counts more.
You feel the pulse from nowhere where you are.

The guitarist fingers in tongues.
They fulfill our dream of many mouths in every sound.
The songs of relapsed Eden realize their perfection from a distant intimacy.

Suddenly you know that the world has an inside in that you're passing through.
This is explicitly not allowed and essential.

yet another happy vampire

Seeing things makes life a dream business as usual.
If neither she nor I have entered this space how did we get here?

A voice imparts its throat, a sentence its hand.
Her greater mind sounds before itself—its raw protects your integrity.
Like life her language likens.

I bathe in a connection but not to come clean.
She muses which leaves no space unlived or not died into.
You forget deep down you want to dance all night.

The music says now is the point where the poem invaginates.
Reading forgets to follow the action story hides.
It makes you want to learn its language to know your own.

This is the future coming up for air.
A poem is lonely for its other reading it's written to know.

Eternity is flame.
I could never say such a thing.

Looking closely you see movement in the word willing to dangle.
A sentence drawing along burns to the touch.

If your ideas are burning a hole in your pocket spend until broke.
Doing everything with the force of dream renders nightmare moot.

Jewels keep hidden by their strange names.

Linguality is language aware there's no way out of realizing reality for real.
Ontononymous the Particular

Work hard or they'll discover you're a fraud, says the Imp.
Judgment stops functioning when it's everywhere.

There's a goddess in my soup was first of all dreaming, then this.
Some things can't be said is how we used to say it, but it didn't help.

Culture high's debate to perfect suspects her motivation's aswim darkly.
Eating apple fear strikes until aware awake.

The field speaks is one of those titular moments with a helping feel of entitlement.
This is how it tells its stories crossing purposes.

Transmission of possibility proves possible.
Grasping the moment stops it.

Hyperbolize the line between us.
Belly laughing rescales the world to never been.

Expose fears with the hunter's art, no, sport, just sport.
There's a door in the gut.

I come back to life as I come back home coming to my senses.
World making wakes to itself new or not at all.

We're here attending being's stopover in the body and mind leaning wilder.
Surrender is now to now in space timed time to time.
At the sound the poem begins.

polypoikilos
matrix in variance

for Arundhathi Subramaniam

It takes time to adjust to a new place between heaven and hell.
You can skip the drama when you're coming from the end.

Declare from the start you're not in charge of the charge in a line of sight reading.
Ruminating foot by foot gives back the sense teething in earth.

Camel walking talk is a sudden option realized slow.

A line bespeaks a universe, scaled through.
Never walk on a curve—the wild side is road center.

Fielding syllables what do you catch on?
Being light lays on top.

Mind knows it all and chooses not to let you know it knows.
There's a cognitive bargain to report further when the time comes.

Undercut your apparent perfection, she said, let light crack.
Willing confusion is a test of sincerity.

Where mind rivers so goes the game plan.
If the fool would follow he would folly further.

The verb steed tells imagination to ride bareback.
Tuning by fire is not a one time thing.

You can't tell it how good it is when it knows another way.
The actual poet is only who lives in poem space.

Opening the matrix of self-torque begins failing.
How many years it takes to find gratitude equal to birthright in squalor.

Sum me up since life dares you.
This crowded page is waiting for your reference beam.

(It isn't poetry until you reorient.)

So much written inside me, so rare to do the actual search.
Writing is not the me who will read this and fail to get back.

Words retain memory of your first use.
They bear no grudges nor do they forget in your lifetime.

Poetry is language finding you over and over at the beginning.

The tantra of syntax works out from my readerly disabilities.
Verbal tonals healing in gut base booming.

Accordingly I have language as I have body.
Neither represents anything not even itself.

Own the motive down to its cell or no light sheds.
The fingered feel of the string tells a tonal timeless.

The image is measured in warmth as in hearth heart sound.
Mistrust perfection just like hypnosis.
Heart fire, stone pyre, and the pen commune in a verb to come.

Every once in a while I eat strawberries again with her mouth.
It tells me one day I'll write human according to the remains.
All promise contains a rose garden it didn't quite mean.

Poetry shocks by your unremembering.
The referencing being beam reads what it activates.
It's not playing around when it plays around, thanks to following the sound all out.

There are choices in the poem but who's here to say whose.
Hands in your pockets! It touches the atemporal all by itself.

The music speaks from inside the curve unending.
This allows for a little death midway in the journey of our line.
Beatrice retained in penwomanship, *reading reading*, the mindful book.

The stronger the idea the narrower the world viewed.
Look before you bite, smell before you reap.

Know the name, see the color.
Hear the idea, know the thing.

Reject the advice to let the mind wave peak.
Find the mind pressure equal to retaining position on a slack rope.
There is a poetics of crafted bird body logic.

The time breeze is kicking up now.
I reshape to take the curves.
Poetic vision is you can't stop making it.

4 *things standing out from themselves*

A true line just now starts making sense and then goes on for the you to come.
Not to get hooked on the next good thing always being there.

The poem knows what it wants to say and I only intermittently find out.
Showing up includes a willingness for blank.

Do you know where you are now? — bad question, as it turns out.
Ideas are so controlling.

In the poem of the real you don't know what's good and bad.
Can't always handle it.

The line is throughscaled.
The feel of the pull of the whole has shapely whirl only when unexpected.

Identity is a tool capable of casting itself off without loss of function.
It's the reference beam in the internal biome and it goes on and off.

I think I'm still me when I forget.
Memory is not the main thing cutting through in the archeology of my beliefs.

Relax without thinking the full mind traffic is worthy of exposure.
The deadliest art is hummingbird light.

I get flarebacks in the poly view.
Splotchlike spaces blanket readerly extent and I glimpse myself on the horizon.

The celebratory self song strings things out that sound me out.

5 *in her dream I'm in the kitchen poking around*

Everything ever said to me conditions me.
History models itself on our lowest common denominator.

What led you to think there's no pickle in your starchart?
No wrinkle in the far look calls out the land of ever old.

The life poem is a factual artifact.
The poet knows why say I'd rather be written.

You know it's your calling when the colors pull back.
Surrender admitting what you've never heard said before.

Intentional dissociation is mad reclamation.
Follow the bouncing ball off the page and into her lap.

A thought has a music mind learns hearing through.
It takes more life in a breath.

Confessing the poem is making me up as we speak.

Standing repented is being turned.
I hear new death in the face anticline.

The sound says what you're saying.
The vision you can't stop making lives you up.

A life works everywhere in its life work.
Even the simplest truth sounds multiple in the folds.

6 *I thought I too must be dreaming but then it didn't matter*

A man is like a pepper:
until you chew him you do not know how hot he can be.
Hausa proverb

If we follow a wild path long enough we see it means to see.
The great study is the way of lapsing order.

The poem is a threshold of acceptable chaos with shine.
A power inheres knowing it's still and ever now.

Meaning is meant to be, seen.
Walleyed things look different differently.

The dream rebreathes the meaning of the words to first use.
Consistency insults the reader.

A bird is quicker than the eye on the fly.
Memory hangs you up so you can't hang up.

Peace is a state of consensual non-lethal aggression.
Who was that masked woman? A word bearing no grudge.

Poetry is language accepting that it's indefensible.

Crazy words in dream make obvious sense, and waking, fabulous nonsense.
I say magic carpet, you think metaphor, now traveling.

The proper study of poetkind is fools persisting in folly.

Whose mouth is muscling inside my lips today?
Only a false appearance of the present can reveal actual presence.

You know it's now when everything conspires.
Virtue is awkward.

In a flash I become everyone I meet in the flesh.
My only hope has been to write beyond myself before the end of the line.

Presence to, from, for, in? Think kaleidoscope. Think merry-go-round. Think facets.
Clown. Haha. Clench of gut. Drone.

Is he after all a Buddhist? Yes I am or not.
Answering is getting me nowhere even faster.

What kind of a person is this? Is he even a kind?
Questioning is getting me nowhere in no time flatter.

I'm a Buddhist when I say goodbye and now this, hello!
Intimacy is unknowable distance highly felt.

Now we fear clowns bespeak deeper danger between hee hee's.
Never said, as it's said, if ever said, probably not, no doubt.

The poem is working in your seeing your seeing another way and not only.
Poet unavoidably creates reader who reads him better that he knows how.

Full disclosure is the genie out of the bottle.

I know it's prophetically now when misreading is revelatory.
This intimacy is closeness risen from the read.

A true thought feels secure enough to mean otherwise.
Written in my lifetime is read in another.

I talk to myself waking or dreaming or not yet never saying don't.
Prioritize thinking clear—tears prioritize themselves.

I no longer resist knowing the dead are reading over my shoulder.
World surfacing has its shifting say here.

I have to reread the work to keep the faith.
Think one thing, space, think back, space, again think tripping up, tripping over, see?

Somewhere along the line you see through to what's not existing before.
Face the provocation of your favorite tune.

There's no such thing as a good line—not for long the way thought leaps over.
Birth aggression never ceases.

Good flow, sturdy flare, pastor's floral.
A power of poetry teaches the delusional they aren't always.

Seeing things has birthright with flair.
Makes you want more even when there isn't any.

Zero point is not without flowering.

9

Pardon my aggressive delight, I said in a pinch.
Don't knock animal sense.
The wisdom of three is that none prevails.

You've been found wanting wanting wanting.
A darker side thinks it has me on retainer.
I see into my dead reading over your shoulder.

Now you know why I brought you here. Who said that not yet me?
Midpoint is thrice wanting.
Language is tone deaf until heard on a curve.

Dates astonish time and again—*back up and say it right.*
Tears prefer tears all around.
This is belly talk in the dark.

Murder is what happens between people you don't know—or maybe not only.
The retainer I'm on won't give a name.
Freak faces from one ha to the nest. *Clown on your own time.*

Violence is passivity gone all wrong.
Flamenco eyes see in the dark. *Duende.*
Love aggresses, violence suicides.

Study your animal.
Your demon is showing in the shooting gallery since life is art.
Not worth a nickel in denial of the pickle.

10 *minddegradable*

I have not made my book any more than my book has made me,
consubstantial with its author.
Montaigne

The whole unfolds in the flow perspective something like cumulus smiling.
Obscurity rouses in the break.

Poetry is aggressive unlike violence.
"Everybody is on a waiting list."
Only remembering the birth to come warms us here.

The knowing tool is self off casting middles.
How I even know I'm here is still on my mind.
I try buying time but it has me already.

We are the membering all over.
Embrace the trace.
It can't have been is how you know it's real.

Think what the mind does when you say be born.
The real is turning you mirroring.
Take the whole world in swinging doors of perception reception.

The whole thing is probably improbable.
Secret is the will to be all out all the time.
Peak means it knows it's there no matter what.

Everyone is waiting on a list.
October 1, a fresh month to watch speeding past.
The eye is the quick bird flying higher.

11 *some like it not*

A good line says you've never read right before this moment.
It lies. Still not reading reading.
It's not no good but good is the wrong idea.

Note how *poem* is having the feel of eternity in a grammar of backflow.
It's drawing on a poetics where defects become as virtuous as the breath is long.
It times as the hour strikes relative and absolute at once—alarm!

Complete sudden ballet in the face signifies character showing with élan.
A throw from the heart a stone's throw from home.
Take things as seriously as they take themselves taking the curve.

The gesture is equilibrational with the edge.
No time to plan in no time.
Writing has no outside while still writing.

We're always on the move out here far from home. It's a bit shaky.
No likes more than you dare think.
Guessing who says these things proves I'm distracted.

Only can follow the track you're on-track on.
Secretly saying talk to me turns on worlds scarcely sensed.
Syntactic nuance is tonal and facial.

I'm on the way to your way is the one thing you feel your way.
The distinction is never free of extinction. You hear a turbulence. Slide under.
What's undeniable is the fact we're both here now, or it's not happening.

A line tried to get through but I was turned away.
The bounding movement you now detect is a species of grieving.

Eluding meaning opens the way to great meaning.
It proves a proverb is a one-line mystery spoiler.

Believing in sudden emergence doesn't require belief but relief.
It is the way it sounds.

It's a dark day to see lighting the way.
Riming registers below the belt but pre-sexual.

Mind slice sharp clean removal better be on the spot.
The authentic barely survives its fraud.

Kiss means not one side or the other.
Similarly you can run your fingers over the curve of the voice.

It follows that it doesn't follow.
These are not contradictions but flashing othernessesß so sorry for your loss.

Lines are steps like the sunflower through the day, my following, lighting ways.
It's something I do to be done while never really happening, just shadows.

On the way to your way I find you here.
A reach in the dark is over an edge we took for skyline.

It dawns, a day has pockets of knowing.
The poem reaching in to find an opening divines leaks.

What if the day is dying for a new language?
Life is one of everything.

A line is by any reach of the imagination.
It's made up of its own accord.

Give judgment a rest.
Cut the attachment with a happy slice.

Where did you get the idea there's no poet at the source, beyond inevitability?
Turning frames accommodate in the Klein house a peculiar way of bottling.

Walls are still falling. Check the rubble.

The poem is an ally in outsmarting my mind.
Mirrors are everywhere woven.

History in a nutshell needs shelling.
A poem is that cracks nuts not only mine.

Aggressive renunciation means loving the ugly and the violent with all your heart.
Murder is too literal.

To recognize writing true not crime you have to find where it has no forebears.
In love means sensing innocent the next line coming on hard.

The people you love are not bad magic.
An all new emotion has nowhere to go but over.

You don't get it until gotten.
Time is on no one's side but a you unknown to you.

Racing to the end slowing is harder than dropping out on time.

We're here to sustain a level.
A gate of any one opens two.

...*communion through brief, isolated, rapid actions*...—L'image!
Nothing constitutes nothing.

A mobile castle is undefended on the spot, and passing.
A poetry is what makes it impossible to conceive a thing.

When you challenge the root the waters know to flow.
Organic is no model.

Consistent inconsistence grows apples diverse.
It's not a puzzle. No answers lure. Loud sharp not knowing next flowers.

It's only tough if you're *trying* while it's telling to tell.
Destiny is just along for the ride, down the incline of the West.

The slide is sacred to its air.
Breathe further.

Contrariwise conceive a thing from scratch in accordance with the itch.
Our countertimes are here right now all along.

It's there seeing it.
No ideas but know themselves as things moving on.

Their heat dangles up.
Once your gut knows fear it always knows.

Dead or alive I get to know the person coming or going in the mind.
It is with some sadness in the reflexive mood that I greet my impersona.

It's not there not seeing it.
Death offers a chance to get to know a person better.

Life on earth builds living earthly.
How can you be sure you're not dead in the present construct?

Reading knows dying anytime through.
Everything orders down to the last drop down.

States, moods, modes, methods foot along like Johnny Appleseed going to seed.
Walking your way you hear a sound that bounds.

Regency's lost agency still sings itself along to tune like yours alone.
Believe you're great for a split second then rabbit over the thought.

Wrought space fires up in place, *hwaet*, how you'll never say.

We are barely local the way we're thinking.
Nothing scratches the itch for the untranslatable.
Accurate records keep safe what no one wants to know.

No ideas in arrears know themselves as wings.
The valences word you counterstreaming with hopes going higher, higher in smoke.
It's a reach beyond forgetting.

The point is to ride an edge you can't prove is there.
Still can posit a pointless point, what fun for an old tearjerker.

So well recorded we're free of taking it to heart.
I take pride in offering no assurances yet it won't stick.
We're still in play.

The music is to sail through the end with all colors flying.
Note the note that slips past less.
They that self-generate least knowing are *still* to know our own.

The sinking ship stays in sync with never saying never.
No help gets with the mystery still unnamed.
There's a point in every way where the slate is self-cleansing.

Possible meaning's surround sound holds you in its swarms.
Hence the lust for a mathematics holding on the wing.

What is the music doing here where the wave crests incalculable?
Enjoying sleights the path withheld in waking all through.

I dreamt light licked my mind like a dog my face or was it a god.

Opening a sensate crack to another dimension comes with sensation in the daily.
Likewise there is a poetics of seeking out the untranslatable.
It starts as longing long.

The neverbefore has no language until now.
There is no such thing as dakini gossip.

My site of completion is just getting started and over before I know it.
I reach out to her only to find no one there but the many.
Any offense is history all over and covering further.

Offending love has a heart of old.
My music isn't. Or not in time mine.
An art of fold tells tales gone cold.

It's the sliced sharp tear through to a you seen through.
I'm in shock at long last time did tell over a dead body.
Feel the terrain lumped up now torn, personial mnemorial longlasting.

It won't let you go forward with history.
The fact of words is a world apart cut through to core after core.
It's how I get here without having been here.

It's personal like a tutorial for absentminded absentees.
The world begins where I think it's ego absconditus at work.
Take me to your reader is all I mishear or miss hearing in the verbal dark.

Why is being here not everything as it is?
Is a wing a will in play?
The deeper the seeing the more it flickers and the light still coming from behind.

What is not mine in time still has my time line live in the present line.
It's to feel for.
Anything able to be said is a matrix of further life hidden by your senses flayed.

Bold saying is not toying with the gods or the dogs, inner or outer.
It's too intimate for boxing.
Overreaching is allowed for cliff singers.

Temptation is not limited to kinds ever known.
Anything ready swings between further and over.

No stopping the crosstalk.
Aberrant branches with worn sheaths verily shout.

Can't help seeming like impersona gossip.
Static in the hearing waves.
Homophonic genomics from tree chatter to blood spatter.

Catch a rhythm like a butterfly.
Agency succumbs to high riding like chariot entrances.
A warp I can't keep hands off teaches dance.

The line is a place to go laying itself yourself out before you it.
A grammar sprays playing the instrument in play.

Imagine jungle reflection.
It flexes its undisclosed gender.

I mean mirror to see her inside myself showing up inflective.
Identity torsion tears away walls insinuating exchange, maybe even place trading.
Listening like eyes on the tips of the palpatorial fingers.

I'm passionate saying what I don't mean to be saying.
Gesture is not time bound but bounding.
The shape is lipped on the way.

It gives and takes tips for a ride where the terrain is real by declaration.
Petals petal like thinking thinks.
If you don't catch it you forget it because it never happened.

Touching down is foundational—we work backwards the words passed through*in*.
Anything occupying this spot is an instance of what has been said *very felt*.
A talking turn takes curving hold. That's how it means what it says. Line flow.

What goes far enough in reflects what wants out.
That it's its own language is meant for you to know before you leave satisfied.
It's *your* falling calling too, the out that's through the door no one uses.

Context is the secret variable.
All the changed mouthing but mirrors a future further.
And every step comes down hard on the gardening for.

Wholly read is never really for.

I wasn't really dreaming, just dreaming I was dreaming.
It showed a shaky middle in the syntax but it seemed to know what it was doing.

I ask why in defiance of my unacknowledged codes behaving on their own.

A reason is a start never over.
Once said it surfaces rough and pebbled.

I walk along as though everything isn't happening under troubled foot.
Thought gets contour with gut feeling getting brainy.

It has to seem a moment's thought because it is.
Poetry proves a moment thinks for itself once said.

Word wills.
Synkinetic poetic rewiring grammars wills for the kill.

Linguality writhes under the strain.
Involuntary crosstalk leaves tracks.

The *status* of the statement clawing for fixing meaning *quo* now in question.

Two rights are wronger yet.
They destabilize my necessary instability.

I sense clambering to restore balance even as the sentence palpates itself en route.
Reading feeling the way along lowers expectations in anticipation of wondering.
Wonder further yet.

21 *feelings have integrities facts ignore*

Enjoyment knows a secret path in waking over the edge.
Ontononymous the Particular

Dislodged speech particles play on nerves for the hotwired bounce.
Shock travels radial wise, slowed saying turning.

Using tracks.
The simpler it seems the more opens out from slack.

All left unnoticed now notices.
The stitching and unstitching is pervasively naught.

What caught notice was making more of itself.
Manifesting means released into being here timely.

I hit on the belief regulating today's body sense.
Credible primal antithesis has words not withstanding stand within.

Crosstalk follows crossing.
Getting across avoids abstracting the thinking to stay with the linking.

Scratch thinking.
We're cutting down on cutting surface.

Thinking life new covers texture like feeling skin.
The realities flicker across with paginal sensation.

I almost got a glimpse of the belief of the hour.
Words have retractable claws unlike cheetahs.
I am suddenly cleansed by my own aggression.

As we move along here take note of the shifting cleats of readerly steps in traction.
There are concepts that further the leap over obstacles and those that grow them.
Metaphors are like mixed drinks, conceptually speaking.

Words withstand erosion by standing with their contraries.
I lament the disappearing month like slipping behind clouds.
Trouble in the poietome where all true words are late in coming.

Am I any more at home if I say *homish* [sounds *unheimlich*] or not?
How can a word you think not exist?
Am I anymore here homing like a bird word?

It's only because questions get us nowhere that they are of primal value.
It's impossible to not believe and of primary force to try.
Language aims to speak true but is not bound to do so.

Glossorealism displays like you say.

It goes so worldly rapid by I'm going freight car hopping tonight.
If you see what I mean your eyes don't betray you for nothing.
There's feeling with integrity even these facts ignore.

A poem is a translation into an unknown language. Idiopoeia.
Did I say the totality of poetic possibilities operating in the living organism's *tongue*?
The only thing belated is the gladhanded word shaking.

Of course I doubt my life work, staying healthy for the nonce.
Seems like impersona gossip where to read translates. Bottom up.

Is it time yet to stop dreading still longing for peace and the grand illusion?

Don't go looking for Dakini gossip or unicorns. Check your motivation.
I'm hearing the theme from life the musical, author impossible.
Where do you go my lovely when you're in your bed?

Flamenco's group trance lectures your work on authorial intention.
I stand inflected.
Is my reader as invented?

The rightness of the next is the core issue of civilization.
I thought I was a robot until I met a nice one, but I was dreaming I was dreaming.
Check your motivation at the door.

Take note of the texture of the floor and the text she wore.
The poetics of compassion resides in the matter itself.
Who ratified the law of cause and effect? I'll sue.

A gift of age is the deeper listening seeping through in background.
The nature of substance is the audio chemical getting from there to here.
Self-less self-creation is a turbulent rubric.

True is what only happens now serving.
It's hard to take.
There's a poetics of not otherwise.

Now that you're dead you know that we weren't kidding when we were kidding.
You can freely love the music in the key of bottom up with own wyrd quotient.

The word wyrd tells a tale with roots in now.

Just imagining the instrumentation listens through.
It induces logorealism in a liquid form.
The etiquette is hats off to the fallen *never*.

Day by day, line by line, body by body, further factification.
The lateness of the hour and its going belief tells me serious.
The world rolls out and the money is counterfeit.

I meant it when I said it then it meant me like light licking my dog face.
Awkward as it is to say right.
The gods make up for lost rime but not reasonably.

No sleep when they hang at the bound.
They know you're there before you do, so hats off.
Tell me I'm great for a split second so I can see stupid. Through the crack.

Everything ever felt still feels.
The long tall song sallies on.
The tangled tongue banks on the mouth evolving new.

Orphée morphée is dreamback with further feed forward.
The mirror you pass through is mercurially substantial.
Keep mouth closed where deadly silver substance talks back.

Character by character tells you otherwise.
Destiny's now destination with its wyrd modification to the root.

Honesty in work imposes no meaning like this.

Idiolectuals should stand at the head of the line stopping here.
The sense of space has a lisp only the actual feet can follow.
Real language structures according to its bent still bending.

Believe only what you don't know.
Ours not to do the why but to let our reasons die.
Not giving is giving up.

The thing said is the actual thought grasping its task.
A turn of the mouth is emotion's motion.
We're here to fray the father tongue.

A verbal messiah is the sword of wording.
It's the way of believing in the object headless.
The image is causeless speaking foremost.

Not giving in is giving out.
We meet mask to mask.
Why keep saying what knows it can't be said can't be asked.

You become what you bear.
Verb destines.
No image stays its thing.

You know it's poietic when the maker startles.

Music is never used up.
Liberation is from line to line.

The clear state in contact lets go images thinking for themselves.
It's startling. Feel its pulse like a hers lost to life.
Try pinning the thing down while it still flies free.

I'm a happy dummy when she talks me though like this.
Her poem is pulling the mouth string I didn't know is there.
I hear me jaw like an other.

It's listening.

Over the line it's speaking for itself by echo.
Mind knows itself on the rebound.
Itself is knowing by grounding, wave by wave.

The line of thinking dies down to turn over.
All of our edges are scraping up against all at once. *I am wall.*
Word mass gets critical at every turn down and echo.

A poem is a canyon large or small.
Depth is physical by sound bounding.
Happiness is numerous inclusive of one. One itself.

Hard as nails bending.
The unhappiest poem is word safe.

Mind's a believing flying machine with Sherlock Holmes in the cockpit.
Who's behind the dark force predefining the range of the heart?
I ask myself out loud yet my head is in the clouds believing flying.

Some narrow is to see what is.
Profoundly making invites indifference to reception.
I'm a stand-up weeping between lines.

Poetry is a near life experience.
Talking funny reminds only undead show no power of past.
Forgive the I talking through me I call she.

I'm faithful to the past in its pastlessness. Or rather hers.
Lear speaks free of his lines. By hers.
It lives to utter deathless by her crossing.

Imagine this is saying the failed saying of before.
Authorization by ineptitude makes a certain sense, alternately real.
Without even being dragged down the lane of identity the deal is sealed.

You didn't see it coming that it shows without consent.
There's no takeaway. No giveback. Where's the fun?
This stands in for a line that can't be written.

Where do we stand? How dare we ask?
It's that sincere tone's skilled deception.
Still claiming to know when the good line's good.
And leave no bridge unbroken.

Bling! muse, your dharma art of talking through dummies.
I say mind, you say tongue, let's let the whole thing show.
How do we handle our well spoken ineptitude?

If my way is the right way I'm wrong before I start.
There are many me's yet I'm here knowing the one of them none is.
To be in the real presence of myself I let the position reverse itself.

Where are you standing in this canyon?
Even curved statement is straight in its parts.
Configure our distance apart and palpate the tone of voice.

Honest work imposes no meaning including this.
No thing said is straighter than receiving.
Scale invariable's dimension variable.

Reading's believing's leaving hearing open.
Poetry is the art of creating the reader.
The discourse is only secondary in the absence of primary.

The Liar's Paradox substrates language itself.
Truth is never already.
There's no before here.

I'm noting nothing just for sound.
Seeing that it goes all the way down reveals no up or down.
I draw myself up into this picture I think I am that sees past.
To follow it is to unfollow everything.

29 *daily incarnation speaks for the people*

Existing throws—you can hear it suffering.

A word in hand is hourglass sand.
Saying it is shape telling timing.
It hits hard like the medium telling dead.

The telling is dead on.
It has no name that the saying is done.
It carves on you.

No compelling. Just swelling falling off.
No true mirror will recognize you.
It suffers readerly dementia inflecting intention.

Life reinvented me strangely today, or was it poetry?
Poet first means the King's lingual taster.
I run from the mirror without moving an inch.

What do I believe today, weathering?
I turned my head to let time pass this time back.
Every moment my self introduces a new subject and I fall for it.

Believing weathers new.
This is living in what it grasps until bleeding in.
The gesture arises not from the past but a trace now in hand.

Thinking over words is hoping to land better.
A simple figure stands different in high winds.

Getting it straight: poet squats in uninhabited lingual outposts.
Whereas systems impede the thinking they channel, resolved that we not here now.

Believing in the devil ages the liver.
Word history means the lingering impact body on up.
It mirrors willing suspension of cognitive competence.

This is over Darwin's head like a *Simurgh* fly-over.
A word is the act of modifying all.
The poem tries to refer as the other's streaming and fails.

Like raga refining cross sound breeding the poem evolutes hearing.
Poetry is not here to promote understanding.
I will myself to the will of the line drawing out.

The line signals reading across the page and we flex.
Talking likes figuring to tell taller.
Cultivating indifference grows difference differently.

Telling time pins it down telling tales like so.
Hooked on the axial disappoints straight saying.
Release into music proves no release.

Everything is straight in its way.
Music has strength of issue.
Doubling straightens strong.

How to hear the mirroring and mind overhead.

Meaning resounds down round itself to fill out the area saying.

Coming up for air overcomes the way back in.
There's understanding like a veil across the face.

The line carries you safely in being carried away around.

The hardened puritan finds the way in through the back door.
Artifice is a sidekick watching out for the semi-blinded borderline impassioned.
Known by the intensity of desire driving the tongue the poem sexes.

Forgive me I'm still learning English at your expense.
We signal problem coverts and send them down the line.
Seek thinking drawing redrawing down line.

Time loops free.
Practicing inhabitory retention language taking up temporary residence squats.
We swivel together setting free between.

Push pull time mirrors our threshold.
The instrument weighs in body.
The weather does our believing.

The fielding feels right at this height.
The work soaks up the life range meaning.
Doing our duty to unnamed things still free of being told what they are.

Life goes on or under the line moving toward the end brings it to light.

The sudden self is seeing itself come upon.
Traumatic history showing you capable of the worst shows real.
The heart opens to let blood flow where it still isn't.

The preverbial line is atemporal in distributing itself any where timing syntax to be.
There's never no how to read.
There is tantra following the points appearing.

The first level psychic's selfie—to divine own mind see through.
Writing is its future taking place as we speak.
Approaching enriches with ratchets.

The trail is not leading but staying between.
We've come and gone from the beginning.
True is what turns true.

The parallel stream crosses here.
No one knows how to read a moment before they do.
Poetry taunts us toward further incapacity.

Access adjacently accordingly.
The line draws its curtains respectfully.
Come upon this thing not knowing is self seeing sudden.

Reading knowhow is nowhere good.
The drawn line is curtains for the past.
Waking is not a desire, it hurts hiding.
Battered heart, cracked heart seen opening through.

Meaning to accept these apologies always lies in waiting.
Waiting can't help lying inadvertent latently.

Species of breathing sustaining lives live tonal.

There is axiality directly said in sheer number of points at once intentional.
And then there is bare saying barely touching down.
It's simple, hyperlocally speaking.

If I can return to this spot it means where it finds.
Thinking raga spares syntax.
I look back to see what blanks have been filled as new ones appear.

The preverbial body waits for therapy you can never guess.
The slightest critical turn sleights attention.
Wake up is an inevitable self-declaring clamor.

The line wants backbone.
A paradox of lying lies at the undercut of language itself.
There's a weak element in the greatest statement signaling health.

Sometimes you have to bite the orange to get peeling.
It's easy to forget there's a ride inside the outing.
I cannot not learn English teaching itself by whatever turn.

This is responding to an occasion not known occasionally.
Waiting instructs where you least want it.
A line makes its claim in residue assembling still.

Time on my hands and heading toward my feet.
The beginning is where you come in.

When I say it's not yet mine it's not yet mind.
Never mind it's never mine from the beginning.

The first level of psychic is psyching self—to divine own mind seen through.
This is the obverse leveler.

The truth is all done with mirrors.
It goes in arrears before it appears.

No time likes the present.
The line gets longer in the end.

Writing on water is harder than to walk here.
To divined own mind be truer seeing througher.

The where is the wonder.
The vine finds out, the wine times out.

Resisting proverbs religiously lingual almost makes hope worthwhile.
Preverbs on the other hand go down on foot, hopelessly.

I am the Red Beard of common contrariness and it's never me you see.
Slash signs for eros' sake.

So saying goes forth only to leave itself behind.

rippling scales

for Elizabeth T. Gray

Sooner or later people tell you back your own stories.
You can see where they eat their verbal lotus.
There's a yoga in just about anything.

Its poem prepares you for the coming crack in text.
It gives rug to pull on out.
Speaking from a time to come counts here apart.

Just ask Inspector Maigret who proves a crack in the wall speaks human.
The survival of the survivors—optimally speaking. The out.
Fight fire with flair.

Even the mirror reflexes to reflect its alien side.
I exploit dreams to honor them however feebly.
The future now is the never foretold.

A poem wishing its truth seeks its imperfection.
The idea that poetry is knowable calls forward its defeat.
Only the Philistine knows its truth in the bite.

Once the poem is known by knowing there is no escape.
The unfolding unfolding itself even as I unfold is syntax to come.
I caught the breathing that made me feel breathed and rushed back here to tell you.

Poet is not prophet as poem is.
Feeling the pulse takes you back to thinking future.
A true saying suppressed by line's end turns back into endlessness.
Love fire with fire.

Future now, never was foretold.

Twos everywhere are hunting for their threes.

Numbers are older within hearing.

Free to not accept the thing that goes before the reach finds its other function.

The antecedent here resides in registration, according.

The note is hearing in its moment.

Faculties are working too hard, it's their job, so perceived, off course of course.

I apologize for not hearing before you before me. Reading doubles.

Reading doubles daring. One more time and it's over its edge.

The definite reference here is exactly how it sounds to itself.

Dagars living forever is sound fact and the India you'll never see seeing you.

A corkroomed autobiographizing poem pulls us into its narrow stream storm.

We'll never believe the atmosphere in this atmosphere.

The mind vibrates around a line shone through.

A same line wants wrack tone.

Questioning quests in advance of answer, guarding.

Fear substrates living welling.

A saying is true outdoing itself.

I admit to saying some kind of something.

By the end of the line a saying is surprised never assuming it's the end.

I can't help looking for the intelligence residing under tongue.
A line sends a message like a current shaking the future now.
I speak to you from afar is language fit to be tied.

Think the thought *the never thought*, a pocket full of sky, say.
It's hard to buy the harder I try. Hard to say.
It doesn't know its own status so why should you. Neither of us is dead, here.

At what age am I myself, even when myselves aren't all getting along.
To mark the question a question misses half the remarkable quest.
It figures itself out as it's going astray.

Raga hands write airing music, literally.
Seeing others from outside skips over the inside easier not seeing.
There's a poetics of world problematics seen from under and other at once.

Each three is a two out of its cage.
We're breaking our connections as the word itself is broken.
It's a discipline yet to come showing up early.

I'm dancing to a tune untuned.
I smell alphabets, I detect the spell foretold.
A wave of hand a word lets loose. There's curve lining.

Letter by letter, thing by thing, self by another.
I keep waiting for a world to know what it knows.

It's only a couple hearing another another come back to itself.

I'm peeling at a different rate today.

Everything doesn't have to pass the intelligence test to know the job ahead.
Heartfelt or talkfelt if truth be told who can say.

Vision sees the world seeing back.
Eyes confuse shifting sense location.
The right verb acts both ways at once.

Never let syntax be as arbitrary as death. Too literal.
Its poetry shows being happy in its nature in its unhappy world.
Vision is what sees its way everywhere.

Line begins in mind, crosses book, alters world.
My way, your way, its way, no way.
Lifeline is poem line knowing it's not knowing linearly.

No ducks, no rows, so they fly.
Doctrine forgets to teach, least of all itself.
Welcome my fit audience and few and getting fewer toward line's endless ending.

Preparing for text crack never fits the occasion.
The yoga current is intervocalic with verbal lotus flourishing between.
The no line further ranging.

Text crack tracking yokes.
If I say so and if I don't, same nonference.
Any morrow is next and beside.

I can only speak as ignoramus unbound.
Foot fruit is the stone stepped over.

No saying fails like the truth.
Longing for supreme leans ahead by a head.

Marchons, marchons, time self-timing.
Music supposes body.

Unlike doctrine confusing learning and stuffing.
Everything responds to everything like it or not so why not lines on their own.

We're talking coming together indifferently apart.
The mind slips by but not unscathed.

A right image speaks for a one all through.
I'm not throwing stones just because they leave my hand.

It's hard to be a believer when it comes from nowhere.
Still can't fathom *Dead men are heavier than broken hearts.*

Yet here we are carrying on like fools in search of true folly.
The first weight is in the hands.

It's no contest.
The distributed dénouement knows no resolution, knot revived, incursion attended.

Apparently my ignorance knows no bounds bounding.

I fell into a mood or the falling world arose in me.
Both, neither, yes.

If it's possible to say it's here somewhere.
I do.

The dying fall is between the words as heard.
And womb is no rhyme of tomb no matter sounding so.

Fall on your me's.
Giving pull to the rug in the way out yokes.

Falling I felt knowing I was born in her leaps.
Sense tactics incurring.

Gender flux is the necessary confusion in making as with angels.
There's a self-realized traffic of pure flex.

Fluid currents are not self-crossing until the incursion.
No need to say sex where the overlapping fits.

No blame of same in the failed striation honors fair.
Joking sounds yoke.

Some syllables stay happy in the fall.
Bound to be their say's long lure.

Duration endures articulate wakes. There are no fakes there.

A wild child's still tearing at the letters laid low.
Her measures unsettle meaning in the hers pointing through you.

You may read it better than I who ends up at your legible feet.
The meaning you don't accept takes its play elsewhere.
Sayings get addicted to being said over and over.

Truth rides bareback in a singular terrain.
What it doesn't say now's in unread reserve.
We return ready for the aroma laid bare.

Substriations of a text to come root like the personalities of a plant.
It says the simple by way of the impossible.
We find ourselves in the sudden between, it lives.

Wait on the momentum with no room for commitment.
The song sings louder than the hearing.
Alphabets spell densest and swift in their arabics.

Source unknown, model unshown.
She rides a tone, fearless with drone.

Identifying the path does not say where you are.
Metaphor means the tough mix is coming our way.
Secret pleasure glanced as tone is tearing at the heart.

Every letter a dying fall.
This means sticking with a music still facing itself.

The poem understands me before it writes me.
The plotting unknotting distributes by swarm and scatter.

I'm so drawn out.

Every non-understood verbal formulation has a future in yours.
Proverb were the religion of language.
Nothing is old under the moon.

Reference lovingly taken even as it disappears between letters waking.
This love bath in between pristine lives unannounced.
No momentum blunts this primarity.

Drawing insatiates.
Already known, strictly untrue.

The depressed demon loves the gut.
There's a poetics of not avenging if you can keep the level.
The semblable imp pervers, throughversing.

Language can't help doing what it tells.
Tension of time types pulses through.
If it gets here it's noiseless.

Dying dies in the saying.
The mystery of poetry is that it is.

Any word close enough has stigma.
Sound perspects elementarious precarious vs. ever nefarious.

I'm just happy we can talk about these things and stay outside carcelarity.
I have not even begun to know what that means but I'm shaking.

The dislike of proverbs drives me over and out.
I'm getting messages from what fronts.

I was ill until the chance to enshrine this very lack dislodged family resemblance.
Reading badly gets me through.

The vocal DNA haunts the ear knowing the tongue is a weapon of choice.
The delay in registering meaning means more than it dare say.

Registration is accepting violable variability.
Every move shakes the cape to inflame.

Flame's the only source of light in the actual present.
The letter burns to the end of law.

This moment needs to spread out.
The temporal mouth opens wider by the instant breath.

No telling what it's saying.
Line wonders where it lays on and on.

This is no place to stop.

There is no season you can call your own.
Arundhathi Subramaniam

Flutter in the wings is no sign of success.
The action at hand is handing itself over as we speak, no fear.
A line draws out its image thinking, so it appears.

Meaning the echo is half heard, half wyrd.
You fall off the end like dream.

The sound differing from itself sounds your other, ever avoided.
Minimal is not less.

Any thinking it's saying right can't help missing.
Always asking what can it mean moves on past.

The habit won't break.
Oneself but drifts away.

Calling it a day is more than it dare say.
The dare like the day is the way it's in the way.

What you hear inside the sound is voiced bigger than itself, but won't say who.
A line goes straight viewed above meanwhile swirling along inside curves.

The list of things not good at is growing by the day.
Incompetence is the last laughed hope.

Unseasonable is hopefully unreasonable.
We look up on low.

What can I say is like the wild joy of not being dead yet?
You think that's rhetoric but it has barely been thought.
There's more than one kind of listening that's not yet a kind.

The right resonance rightens the body and live body registers lightening.
The joy is hard core tonal turn.
The level shift in materialarity is word turn for reseated physic.

All new stuff is excitatory fact sensing.
Instant jargon is thinking it more than once.
The language herefrom is bargaining with the invisible.

If it spoke at all it wouldn't know what it's saying.
Meaning is for listening with.
Some meanings release the inner cello still audible in the name aloud.

Saying your name can't be recorded from outside.
At the sound level poetic means an exalted sense of your own import.
It takes getting thrown off sounding your own name to reposition identity.
The strangeness, the fallen out, the caught over the edge, a sudden foursome.

The thought here is no longer mine but traveled where I am to be.

I'm not thinking clearly therefore I'm not quite here.
Identity is what you can never be right about.
The tense is the intensity of the tension.

Minimally music knows it's real.

Putting your mind on the block is decisively metaphor.
Likewise cello is a human voice displacing inside.

This is what we go to poetry for, outing interior surfacing.
Showing it for what it is the first of infinite last times.

If you ask long enough it will say everything always.
The true tune never gets to the end.

The hunt for the hole reflects the lack that drives it.
I end before the poem always.

These are not lines but strata of rising again now.
It feels like crawling on the outskirts of your own sense of things.

The weight of a word holds down the house under siege.
And sentence ages the Age.

Names have needs.
Nietzsche mind is further history down to the actual current.

Memory in the flow retains the changing continuous core acting.
You try to get the feel even as it feels itself for the first time.

The landscape is from the train window of thought.
It's passing before our eyes through our hands.

The mirror reflects further when you let it, double dare.

Say it again, Lamb.

I repeat ad nauseam there is no repetition.
A signal disperses in desperation of positive indication.
How much poem saves?

And how many senses in the urge of the poem to come?
A line displaces the poem unwritten.
Language never stops learning filing itself down to fit.

Not talking about itself talks endlessly back in.
Agency is go-between.
It feels fuzzy so fine its logic faces around.

Inside here nothing stays lost.
The endlessly longed for knows where to find you.
Feeling yourself alone is the musical surround.

Lingual yoga stretching from the core leaves nothing behind.
Mysterium injunctionis tremens literacy.

Filling still.
I feel on call.
The line is on my trail.

The poem rethinks itself with or without me.
Flaw sources taste.
So revealing is the peeling.

Recurrence is the trace of something returning to itself.
By its nature it asks you in.
It feels like going back by a twist of the life link.

No such thing nothing thinks.
The very act reclaims living current the world is giving away.
Just feeling directional is roadworthy.

The impulse to speak in the raw sets the course.
It helps to expand no outcome.
Thinking forgets what it is if it ever knew.

Poetry the calling in a long dark hall recalls itself.
It's no way to think from a long way off.
Life re-declares itself every unending moment.

This sounding forward beats the ground with blood pulse minding.
As fact as it gets between you me and the earth.
Seeking waking light mind aims being the only member of a set of no members.

Longing's ever its length.
Believing's not telling it's the bastard child of truth.
Anti-metaphysics is a metaphysics, notes the imp of glee.
At the end of the hope line reading ceases knowing it does know what it is.

Dip into the swirl of sudden certainty.
Teaching is inside everywhere.
There are no heroes outside the poem.

Language is off its rocker again today.
Rare roarer rears harmonious.

Shock is the state of being more present than you dare.
Every statement risks meaning less than it says.

Remote lives are far worth living.
Depart from stillness to be sure.

Devil's work is angel's work veiled by lapse.
Denying what I feel is business as usual trafficking in pleasance.

It takes me from gag order to gag reflex by way of verbal gag.
And so much more than seeming to say.

Stop trying to make your mind up, I keep saying to myself, but I'm not listening.
Bad news it gets personal even in the middle voice.

Inventing mind vents time.
No taking back extravoluntary sublime.

Getting reborn departs from stillness loud and clear.
Therefore the poem cannot escape being my hero in tough times over dark seas.
It's about finding its place as it steps on over.

Gender left to itself speaks in the intraphatic voice.
Will is not a dick, she assures.
So sees the word problem from the salty inside.

Poetry finds the rocker language loves.
Its musicality is oscillophatic.
Disorientation is a rhythmic occurrence.

Poetics means it matters how you get there and not much more.
Unless you hear otherwise it never comes to matter.
How many missteps per unit does it take to invent dance.

Where is the gain when you can't say gain but do anyway.
"Everything is made of emptiness, and form is condensed emptiness." (Einstein)
The word relative is relatively useless beyond a certain point. Swim.

Teachers plagiarize things and brightly.
Where are things not and yet so vivid.
Music is local or not at all.

Language that can't catch itself can't get caught.
Most vividly it can't think what it is.
Happy orientational rupture in the ripple outward as we speak.

The music is what slices through.
It's never heard you before the very moment.
The poem is language coming to.

Where is the gain in the presence of the endless ending.

A living thing steps out of line from the present perspective on.

17 *forgetive options*

Reheated cabbage kills teachers.
Juvenal's "Seventh Satire"

We mark as we go, wolfing worlds.
The line is on my tail.
I rail until I pale—*cramming cramboes!*

Life jests where mind nests.
I get testy when tested.
When mind changes same changes.

Suddenly it knows I've never been the same.
It differs from itself seeing itself.
Once the personal motivation is abandoned moving out brightens.

Will tightens.
(In)transitive is a twofer.
No action is safely singular.

No singular action is safe period.
Losing all companions leaves the bearable behind.
Holding out holding hands near.

You don't believe me without attitude.
Don't you wonder if they said what they said they said?
Hearsay hears say.

Do you miss me? poem asks poet with imp of perverse force.
I'm out cold before you know it.
Time to forge it.

The sense of being seen through shows us our lens nature.
I'm someone else's psyche is how poiesis mind gives feedback.

Welcome to the waking dead lottery and the chance of your life.

You can't say all the poems. No matter who's talking.
In these woods the voice you hear is never quite your own.

Saving time like saving souls is drawing out pulses.
Truthing's the unforeknown blowing over. All out.

No talk of poetry but it talk itself.
Check the opportunism of thinking a next line.

The real music is the one hearing one is elsewhere.
The ethic is not persuasive.

All shots cheap like all thrills guarantees now wakes.
What's driving what's showing.

The beyond of saying spirit is the unsaid.
It's not a trap knowing no way out or back in.

Retro-auditive music swims backwards while you're facing.
Meanings pool. We wade in spades. Hallow swords words.

The poem is language hearing all round.
Just like that it knows.

Never to fit fully inside your body or your poem is what is called samsara.
Names are wrong from start to finish.
You forget the poem remembers itself before you, and you don't know it in time.

No time is not an experience, spatially speaking.
All language estranges the sense of identity.
And these are the very things that cannot be said.

Worth speaking.

You can't possibly know how stopped short we are here.
The mind knows it's tracking down the absolute in its singular incline.
It can't resist the faith it's here.

Minding being stuck in here is not ideology.
Only the signals from outside peripheral vision make replete.
Round being seeks sound surround.

My head is turning and I may be missing the message, meaning sign of the times.
Bliss is a practice it's already blissful to wish for.
Stones wait for silence to speak.

Suddenly the primary other reality is climbing the stairs underfoot.
This seems to be going on for centuries.
I wait at the bottom.

Poetry enhances your permeability.

False start is a species of birth with certain protections.
Here is where I come to see my life as experimental directionality.
The dénouement of sustainability's where untied we stand.
This is like learning to walk all over.

Space times out before the end of the line.
Line of course is metaphor like continuous comparison of beginning and end.
They conspire and no competing, for what's the rush, to mean.

The line pursues its own trans relation.
We hyphenate wherever we can, mindfully, in apt avoidance.
Like taking sudden numbers as approval rating subtle interventions.

Why the obsession with three?
The poem has no idea.
It proves misunderstanding is normal.

Walls are lasting failures.
Like three a god insinuates to inseminate.
The laugh that puts you with child.

Walls are delusionally sustaining.
Going against nature procreates original.
Hilaria seed. Hortus conclusus with wild vines.

Split a gut to rupture a rut.
No matter how common the word fuck the primordial act shines through.
The belly mind breaches the body bonding.

Say she sings to a higher flower.

There is no authority to read right.
Deuces and rights are wild.

Support is not offered.
Stones are clearly waiting. So am I if I say so myself.

Indicative means wanting it to be true right now.
Waiting is self true to a fault.

It is said poets say the same thing all life long but what if it isn't the same same.
Feeling excessively frugal.

Dirty jokes mind fuck.
Agency obscured at behest of Eros.

A poetics refuses to wink at the reader anymore than yourself in the mirror.
Look on. And on.

Blackening funny bones lie by the road as if speaking true.
I'm reading into the thing the thing's not being a thing.

Theurgically speaking scratching out your message excites the medium.
Say Greek readied for Homer as English for you still unknown excites the unborn.

We're crossing a line here.
The action is out of bounds and we're stepping on the cracks.

22 *alarmed exit*

A devil who speaks to you is a devil worth speaking to.
Robert Kelly (on the phone, 1972)

The stage is on the line as the curtain goes up on another other world.
We're not where we said we would be.
The voice you hear is thrown from over there.

Whoever said there was no continuity between non-continuous dimensions.
I'm reading into the poem the poem's not being a poem.
We can move these objects around because we see them non-objective.

No act of language is translatable to another act of language without loss of license.
Otherwise how are we here together.
We think to know no show.

Travel a path enough, it finds your way.
The tongue takes on lean.
We're wound.

It means what it says.
Wounded and wound up.
It reads you that you read it. A certain bounce, rebound.

Language teaches itself our ways in lines with wave.
It can't possibly know where it's going and why would it.
Its going knows it. It sounds out. Follow sound out with suprasegmental resound.

The dénouement is the unwinding sentence scarcely spoken.
It's the naga trick, the long white snakes we don't dare say exist even if they did.
It oddly forgets to outdate itself on the way out or in, even.

Hard to get the mouth around the thing that must be said to hear beyond this.
Naga nature nurtures under the very ground here. For instance.

Theophantic murmuration, hmm.
Mouth must open to hear to say my murmur messages.

Poem stutters for good.

If a dakini showed up in here the mind would feint.
The magical moment is unjustifiable.
The dance of tongues is in tongues. Born that way. Non-self-referential, even.

Poem world shifts are scale invariable, ever ruptural.
The naga under the willow tree is of indistinct dimension.
Its mode of existence is self calling into question with weather.

Question has fit. Like any far-flung flight phantasy.
How much do I fit into my question if fit's small.
Just so much force gets through.

Meaning swarms with uncanny accuracy.
More theophantic murmuration moving so slow you can't detect it.
Sound the alarm to get the meaning out in time.

Out in the air, word birds account for a feeling in the belly mind.
Time spreads, music thinks.
Meanings of a weather stick together. Airs cluster.
I hear them hearing themselves.

Wondering how it feels to get out in the air has brought this all the way here, phew.

It's further evidence of the long scratch.
Keeping the focus turns tricks for the momentary believer.
Torquing turns take your mindly breath away for its own good.

I admit we need a corner to work a good ear longing to be free.
Feeling that old black magic is one blackening word at a time.
Reckon it only happens in the dark lifting in nanoseconds.

Under syntactic tongue a question is having a fit.
You feel the vibe in the lip service.
This is the corner of which we seem but dimly aware.

Swear allegiance in the slag.
Understanding this wants control.
Now the mouth is spoiling the math.

It learns reading new at the reader's expense.
The line touches down and down further.
Thought reaching ground still sustains the swarm.

Every new turn shows a poem's way's long in hiding.
Skipping seduction like stones across the lake. Wave bounce.
Things take a turn at the break.

For self's sake a mind's in play.

The content of writing's what needs to be.

Poet is destined to spin.
It's the habit befalling fails to habituate.
For we talk in circles to entrench a matrix we fall back in.

So one pass through and the poem's a you.
We is manyer than one dare say to unaccountable *you* still reading through.
The content of voicing is who needs be.

Action at a distance re: number of lines down page pages across.
It matriculates other wheres.
Swarming possibles to be believed holds sense of identity spun.

A poetics of healing asks what you're willing not to know to be known through.
The hand glides over the verbal curling wavicles.
It feels adrift but it's got grip.

Learning to listen over time likens flying over icy waters.
Crackthrough, *durchbruch*, breakout, breech surfacing.
Forge it to forget. *Ofer wathema-gebind.*

Interletter/interlip the split calling talking back.
The science of literate hand likens nano timing.
Scale invariance gates poetic resonance a way through itself.

Past present implies grammar future perfect ready but for the lag to be.
Some things said still say the more my mind is yet to conceive.

The more invisible the godly the more to fear.
Ontononymous the Particular

Getting in touch with origin is another act before you scarcely a fractal away.
Meaning to say is the sound back through where forward is an unknown.

Authority by sheer drive is one foolish persistence worth rethinking.
The core thing laboring to be said dreams of catching up with itself.

Listening the old words are the hearing just over there.
There's no escaping dangling modification, for undeniably we're still on the line.

How to know the thoughts thinking from those not yet.
Always wanting to think the good thing would mean we're in the wrong place here.

Here is an echo of itself as much as you're aware.
Understanding is not the forefront of intention except mutually.

Easy to think that because there's two of us we know what we're saying.
We have pretensions in common so we can say as much.

We have yet to step in the matrix of our own making even once all out.
You know what it is to change your mind before the end of the line here and now.

Saying anything right finds a trail to be.
It's only known by its fateful music.

Its effort gets others to believe about one what one can't believe about oneself.
The invisible's not less so once made visible.

loosening grip the more to hold

Just now I discovered it's not I deciding the status of what passes through here.
Refrain along with me like a coffee break justly going viral as we speak.
The wobble in my ways cannot be justified.

Sentence equals event with trace eventuality.
Touching you I'm touched beyond recognition.

The micro impulse surges under the radar.
Spreading under parts lips differently.

Human kind cannot bare very much skin, in the game.
Nails in the crucified are not the agony.
Today feels Jean Genet writing my inevitable mind drama.

Sarah laughs to birth proves bible humor.
Ancienter reference sacralizes full frontal lobe.
You get gut smarts with gutter mind glory.

I doubt I can do this makes sure the doing.
Head off base submotives by eating them raw.
Fight for stone, vine and sex intelligence in the right to be or flee.

Take it straight, take it not, your take, now mine, in the know's no show.
Laughing seeds even palling needs.
Forgetive empty set unsettles the set-up.

One hand in another remobilizes selfsame.
I understand you only as you change me.

Looking into the eyes in the photo who is seeing who.
Sophia ships out right bespeaks a sense of second sight.

Does she know what she does to you just letting you into her eyes?
Felt pure outcome's forever.

Language under this kind of pressure is extra voluntary.
That's a positive and a negative thrown out indifferently, with heart.

I ask the line to steer me right knowing what I no can do.
The ethical hand talks beautiful.

The girl in the photo never tires of seeing through me.
Not only poetry makes you feel exposed.

The gods know you want to know them by the sense of beauty.
Your mode is their mood.

There is an extrasensory dimension of even the handiest line.
Proof is it compasses correct.

An extravoluntary handshake metaphors by internalizing verb.
You get the meaning indistinguishable from the gap, personally.

Wording like thinking status erodes in actual use, so it means it.
Even with its pants on fire sentience speaks true while bending the note.

The harder lesson's alarming to learn.

This angle the mirror reflecting further sees she stares me down.

Compressed verbals tell tales on illimitable fools.
Spoken tongues don't break for mammals.

Tell me why the mind kills randomly in revenge, O Muse.
The poem cannot refuse an open corridor however dark (I fear).

Never to stop where the hot breath of contrary ways warps saying.
The music torques decibels at still unheard levels.

Believe in marvels born of marveling.
Hyperspatial elves lead to no conclusions.

You cannot believe someone is talking this way so it's safe. A real poem?
Enlightenment rationality grumbles in background where I curse illimitable gulphs.

Can't help declaring the absolute open, at least on the outbreath.
Spaceships are metaphors for metaphor.

The daimon holds back what you give never.
It talks with what you give it.

Verbal straits and marveled gates are absolutely open.
"A closed mouth gathers no feet" is all relative. [Douglas Taylor, 1957]

And yet her face tells all you will to say.
Thus a life learns how it's bent, resounding.

A good title is a set-up for disappointment.
Music remains before.
Soul and mind do the talking on one's behalf, once accepting their own distinction.

Mood mode dangles extra voluntary.
Not having thought it is a virtue of the instant at next. Now this.

Mind dreams up soul in its night.
Who can say when.

Music enters the bones before you know your hearing births.

Undersaying is knowing all words verb.
This is the stratum peaking.

Mystery is it never stops.
The poem is cutting away.

Soul is mind dreaming before existence.
Even thinking it is evolutionarily grammatical experiencing.

It knows at the point of no remainders the line ends.
Singularity naming the zone of absolute retention defines precious.

Speaking evaporates hot in its matrix.
Anything is inseparable at the level of knowing itself.

Soul tells mind it sexualizes effortlessly.

Varieties of poetic danger include yourself imprisoned in desirable form.
An action on the scale of the raw field is listening to it telling in all its voices.
I'm offering evidence my incarnation continues to complete my incompletion.

The awakened mind in its field is neither living nor dead nor not.
Next writing means for those thinking everything to the edge of beyond it.
The alternative emphasis is the meaning you least suspect.

The chameleon saying mimes my mind.
Apologies for self-indulgence in revealing this, whoever's it turns out to be.
Some things never seem familiar like words that never remember you.

Dragon mind idea configures dragon being configuration itself.
Impossible to escape the fantasy of knowing the fantasy.
Limen is the space of awareness between time and no time, so spoken.

Proof that a poem *turns out* to *be* is that we're getting in deeper, not out.
Not knowing what's happening leaves no alternative to what you're saying.

Believe neither what you see nor what you don't nor anything said about it.
My existence tissue speaks with forked tongue.
Everything is life threatening.

Dragon is scale invariance in action.
Thinking larger poem space producing its other side
Line after line, life after life, no remainders but pulse.

Even now never all in the river of time oozing past into future now, backflowing.

We can't handle the open.
Not knowing who I am is the present instance.
How it means depends on how many ways you think it can.

Skipping the issue of brain which retains historical impact's not finding verb timely.
It also depends on how much time you're willing to give now and then now.
Give *now. Give* now now.

How you read it is how it reads in you.
Skipping the issue of how much squeezes through begs really begs the questing.
Emphasis added on request. *Have emphasis, will travel.*

One issue's not skipping the question of agency while subjecting subject to pressure.
How can we not do this is the obvious question.
Line distributes subject because it says so.

We let reality take hold on the wrong side of the bed, the right side.
Juggle the issue and watch what it says midair.
Everyone in the cage speaking at once puts pressure on the right.

We in editorial are calling this scaling up, out and over.
Subject absent until provoked.
Minimalist grammar for maximalist expression. This is practice. Remember.

The poetic matter has come here to experience itself anew and newer yet.
Syntax by intensities, the cut, and the rattle.
The relationships are variable scale invariably.
I can say something real and no one will even know.

A line is only a line giving its teaching.
Shut up and drive. For instance.

I'm letting the cat out of the raga.
Word desires into being.

Word coterminates with thing said to be.
Hard endings, soft manners in twos.

Before bodying word urges.
Looks to the past for anything but authorization.

Two sides of the coin, in hand, noun/verb, now flip it.
It tells the future, like Mesmer.

A coin alive, an inch right, an instant left, and back again.
The syntax of petroglyphic cave is maneuverable tunneling mindful space.

I know in a moment aware life is channeling my body.
Saying it reconnects it to the engendering urge.

A portrait still born under old glass still flows.
Anything possible to register here thinks beyond sense.

Everything is life sustaining in its turn.
Still checking back to primitive primeval primordial villaging with trepidation.

Any thing said flickers true like nothing else in turning key.

Speaking as hostage to the mind, poet tortures language that tortures her.

According to the physics of history insanity rises.
Duende is the higher intimacy of the prey.
An action by field lets the whole thing die in your arms.

The projection is the lead back like yo-yo in ruins.
Archeologoic gnosemes image premetaphoric.
The difficulty in sustaining one's view in dark times proves historical.

The image longs.
Satan falls upward.
Thinking tries on, and on.

Historically language holds its corruption within.
Keep it to yourself is not optional discourse.
How do you figure a figure undergoes subtraction?

Who can judge what has no forebears?
Writing desires you off-center the more to be what isn't.
Symmetry is a connection mode turning mood.

Alarmed exit awakens.

A touch is irreversible.
Linear distribution subject touches down on a reading mission.
This is the invisible river we share not entering once only.
One day it takes you personally—incursion/bride out, you flip.

flayed flaws
& other finagled opacities

for Charles Stein

1

the line not spoken

L'état d'esprit, c'est moi
Hypocrite lecteur

Mean me in circles, I said upon waking, unsure of the sound I was hearing.
"An assemblage is an exercise in difference seduced into going straight," said she.
The feedback is coming from below.

I admit to missing the symbol in the baby carriage.
This is neither satire nor satyr.
I am neither you nor the poet.

Then it hit me, like you I can't say what it isn't.
It's fair to assume that this is progressing toward a point, like life, career, reputation.
History can only say *this too happened*—the rest is poetry.

I believe it fair to aver that we have come to the right place.
Nouns are verbs in hiding.
It's the law of the land or a flaw in the sand, but no politics before coffee.

I could not possibly know that the poem is real all the way down.
The tune releases us from thinking how we know what we know.
Poetry is an art of the double life. (*Nouning verbs hiding.*)

The line swerves to save the child crossing blind.
Insisting on meaning will only keep it at bay.
We are more and never the three shall meet.

Dark desires in self luminous manifestation reclaim our missing parts.
Suddenly I saw my life as a study in request.

Today is the day for polishing the inside of our cave, and no harming the glyphs!
Unfortunately the poem is holding out on me at the reader's expense.
I'm writing to change its manners.

Sense of beauty is the other name for health in the neighborhood.
Reclaiming the missing parts means following the sparks.
When knowers collide there are no winners.

The mystery is needing numbers—hooks, temporal or not.
Symbols die with my permission or not and take rebirth elsewhere like it or not.
I can barely be here, I can scarcely not.

A line has drawers with intimate spaces where reading reaches under to pull out.
The feeling tone is in the hand and the heart matter touches.
Dare we feel what these fingers know—quintuple dare. Now double it.

The message is the bounceback.
Catch.
Hands off the music.

The line is a meridian.
Heat of the hemisphere as discriminating placement says everything about sides.
Against the law to cross the double line, hence the need for a double life, semblably.

Imaginary lines circle the planet so long as I attend.
Had to bounce my ball straight across to stir up enough trouble to mean.
Even lousy confession or foppish faith holds the line against chaos better than I.
Fore!

The poem gives, the poetics takes away.
There are no Buddhists.

Holding against the line is child's play.
No more bad style, even less good.

Arrogance is interfering with the poem's itinerary.
Listen, the Rudra Veena is playing my rune.

No missed meaning intended.
Request thematizes itself in the very act of being inevitably.

Certain kinds of accuracy are frankly boring.
There has never been a single Buddhist from the beginning of time.

The poem knows to serve as atemporal hideout.
Clock time, body time, dream time, sex time, no time, optionally.

Oar-strokes hypnotize the lake flows.
Lazybone syllables turn in the poem's sleep.

You can't miss the archetypes.
Art is not covered by identity.

I got hurt but then lost track of which one of me it was.
My sense of self comes on like linear distribution rune subject.

The line writes out as if knowing no end in mind ever ends.

Impossible question: Who are you?
In non-binding sequence a poem is working me in the hard way, same *out*.

Her sentence veered just when you thought it meant something.
Just missed me.

The self shell holds out reflective light.
Everyline a drama in monologue all its own unnamed.

In this way an impersona invents itself and takes me in.
Studying my life asking where is it?

Whatever it is it's oldfashioned like an LP with truer sound in a real world.
The idea that there are degrees of reality is way overblown.

Is today a dress rehearsal for the rest of my life? she asked.
Identity takes practice.

The beginning whole is the only whole to end up here.
Story's ever on the hunt for spare parts.

E.g., a Buddha with Taoist feet means we're in China now long ago.
Does exemplary life imply that a life is an example of something else, or not even?

Can't help amusing rime using time.
If you give an easy way in you leave an easy way out.

The poem reveals according to time served.

Time escapes me.
Loving the color the feel the appeal blankets far.
Dakini or she who signals ahead it's me on an outside chance.

A mature work is a relic in its own time.

The hardest rule of thumb for humans is *no faking.*
Ordinary's code for deep confusion.

The poetics of the hard way in or out involves a kind of baptism.
It's impossible to escape the problematic of momentum for it distributes by field.
I can't find the poem on the page.

Is it not obvious that a core strategy is zero tolerance for the obvious?
Fleeing from refugee world the joy takes refuge in mind cracks.
Radical rupture of words between eternity & now passes healing mouth song first.

I believe everything at some instant of the day, getting from place to place.
My poem knows the back way to La La Land having grown up next door.
Impossible request: *Be straight with me.*

The preverbial censor removes *Flame not that ye be not flamed.*
Memory fails from the start.
The universe curves out of primordial lust, remembering fear decenters flair to flare.

Every moment written serves ecology gone eternal.

Names failing to name earn their naming truly, the hard way.
No more missed meaning, for where would it go.

I didn't name her Sarasvati, they think they did.

Her veena plays me.
It hit a light center lit newer many lives at once.

I construct with destruction lite, trying to stay ahead of the swerve.
Standing on the right to be tilts.

The practice is the present point in syntax plus don't get you nowhere.
It takes its cues from you don't knowing.

This is a method of heart flutter taking flight with what won't float.
Language knows this way but won't tell us.

Prophetic reformed fakery—just thinking that throws open cabinets.
The question is what gets you up the back of the moment.

Lily spires. I think I'm seeing out from saying it.
Rhythmics in arrears catching up the first time ever.

We flatter our focus and he saw that it was good.
I love your fingers. I love your mouth. But not together.

Passengers are requested not to leave their minds while moving beyond.
This vehicle makes stops at High Romanticism with destination unknown parts.

Right here where we are her being is practicing itself.
Every sign you're on target excites.

We live in evil times loving the earth to death.
Who's speaking but the responsible.
We are they who don't yet know how to ask.

Studying my life asks where is it?
My foolish ways are smarter than me.
The line is the mode of the moment meaning more or less.

I know it's my work when I'm feeling at home wiggling free.
The only rule is don't tell it what to do.
So long, so long as there are pages turning.

You know it's alive when it reads you back.
How otherwise did I know it was thinking that thought.
The poem is my language looking into me, its creation.

I am a B- student of this very sentence.
I'm working my way up to diagramming a sentence yet to form.
And watch it flare.

By the time you know enough to name it it's ashes & diamonds.
Thanking someone/-thing for this good fortune but thankables won't stand still.
Asking only basic questions so long as my ego can bear the pressure.

Finding your register signals a place, where to now?

The emotion told true is no longer itself.
Language owns.

It's here to get situated.
A peace in the voice shakes foundations.

Even if it didn't ask we're here to think in difference.
Suddenly I was layering the sentence back into my chest.

Hospital is the other end of pretending.
Passing water in the street fast driving listens fast.

Fact: I am alive and well between syllables.
A poem thinks difference differently.

Doubt is always there to be had.
Must be a poem if it strikes a current setting it going beyond that.

Opinions are eels.
Gazing doesn't know who's doing it.

Voice, wind, wording, listening to the music he heard that it is good.
Is a rainbow only like or does it look the fact?

But this opinion will not be held.
Doubt and belief are dance partners after sundown.

Existence leaving itself out at its own expense learns its value.

There are conditions for unconditionality but we'll keep going regardless.
The words distract from meaning to make the mind safe for truth lodging.
What we're hearing is the sentence whispering to itself between syllables.

Things come in threes like it or not.
I'm trying to kiss the seconds with swift lightness as they fly.
The tyranny of symbolism is in making us want it.

The times are pretending to be evil again.
Words throw their symbols at you from undesignated directions.
Knowing I'm shown in my handwriting I get nervous.

Like defending the defenseless this is useless to advantage.
Bad leaders are spears in the bleeding side, tyrannically speaking.
The same words get friendlier on the quicksand page.

I reached for the thing but it was still dreaming.
A poem's future depends on the pool pooling before it.
Finally felt for a split second the pleasure of appreciating one's own handwriting.

Quick thinking is a shear thinning non-Newtonian fluid discursus.
I'm writing by eye to get to the bottom of it.
Eye has bounce according to the fingered word alight, the page, the page on fire!

The poem takes you by the eye and it feels by the throat.
The point is to live by way of cracks.
A time to curl up between actual unaccountable words never before known thus.
Naked enterprise always only.

Not selling is political and inconsistent.
Tiling my narratives creates a surface to pass over retaining.

Dream realism graphic image density incomplete sentences mumbled key words.
Poets are not consenting adults.

Lower animals don't wonder why they're doing what they're doing as they do it.
So no poetry.

True standards never meet.
Civilization can't deal with the three souls in one breast.

Conscious deviance drives syntax.
Hilaritas is where it looks back through holding tight till crying out.

It lights a parapropaedeutic finger within the page.
Bouncing tale for following.

A principle of scale asks reading to carry this pervasively in a life longing longer.
It teaches entry by the side door, followed by a committed leap.

It demands a mind on all threes in the body wandering beginnings.
Let's cut some grooves and groove some cuts.

I paralogize but the principle is paraconsistent.
Passion down grammar's running on empty.

Contraries speaking contrary truths smile the same smile.

Double agency is a fact of life perplexing and then there are three.
No meaning is ultimately missed but follows along on and on.

Which handheld frame are we speaking in and about? Selfish question.
Greek was as ready for Homer as English is for me still unknown.
Seeing in threes reorients the two hemispheres.

Just kidding proves justice is kinder than thought.
Reality blanks out when you get it.

Imbricated tellings give every side a one up.
It's who pokes through to who(m) hears better.

Inferior practitioners wet behind the fears need all the help we can get.
Look who's talking. No one I know.

Writing self shrives.
Sitting on the sidelines a music is imagining in me.

The only safe accident is impossibly accidental.
I hear space in every note.

The unfolding line throughscales .
Fit is not preference.

The guard is at the door tells by the music of knock. Please enter.
Thinking itself now the bud buds there saying when.
Nostalgia for the thought you could never think.

12

We're fresh out of sames.
At the cleft turn left.
Otherwise we're written in no time round.

This thinking can be distinguished by tough music green fuse driving.
All narrative forces the issue.
No on.

The same words cannot fall out of the same mouth the same.
There's bounceback and furtherbounce.
On their own poetic ideas wear out instantly.

Went to the other side of the tone and got scratched.
This is a poem assessing the space left in a darkened world.
It makes tripping over what you're saying look elegant.

Groping the surface of reason, *I speak in season.*
Any variation in saying the saying risks saying the more.
And outs an operative contrary belief system we live by birth to death.

Like my mother said I want it both ways (at once!).
I didn't know I was here till I knew we were here together.
Saying so's defining us before our eyes.

Variability of meaning in the night tongue is advantage by day in a darkened world.
What an exciting mapping device in the service of excitable mind.

Finally beginning to get the hang of it.

Poetry has appetites.
A come and a go of same.
Then comes the swing of it. Makes three.

Like making tea for thee like three for two.
It all depends on the break and how things fall, one and all.

Then comes the brake on it.
This is not a progression but an altered sensitive subtraction with excitement.
Poetic ideas have a half-life.

Too little attention has been paid to incommensurable logic in daily life.
Yes there are no same lines for yes there are at puerely imaginable angles, or angels.
They come from nowhere whence we return.

Buddha never say shoulda.
We are in hot pursuit of Klein Bottle Scripture.
It starts sentenced to rupture.

If you thought it you got it.
I speak an affect for a reason.
You're understanding but you can't tell what is poetic understanding.

It never lets you go.
Raise high your antenna, poet!
Pluck that live fucker from the aether, Bertha.

I admit everything, it's a fold, got the feel.

The metaphor is the hand dealing.
Here we sit calmly at the center of the cyclone.
Remember only the immemorial.

Making a list of words no matter how many times I look up still can't say I know.
Timeworn terms shorn of memory.
What I mean is they never seem to remember me when we meet.

Lily of her valley namely proves dolphins speak intimately.
This could be a translation, for instance, target language to come.
Think ocean, think scale, think folding tongue.

Barely any believe in their own accord.
All balls curve.
Where there's half-life we start with the present and move to the absent.

Any unapparent logic incommensurably guides us along hoping we'll find it out.
Some hear in the cracks the sound saying most needed things.
What's beyond speaking speaks clearly in the between.

Only misunderstanding understands it is so.
Truth is a non sequitur like realest things living.
Satisfying is coming in the unsaid saying right on through.

Meaning has a shelf life.
The proof is in the routing.

Today I got in touch with being unborn again.
I've been finding myself in the middle of a vast sentence self knowing in the spread.
The poem is the place where my identity knows itself otherwise—looking big!

It seems I am that by which the field knows the point, as if there is one.

The author didn't die but shifted her dance's self-obscuring hide-&-seek availability.
Her language coming strong owns my eros.
I didn't know the gun was loaded.

Karma is the effect my mind has on the world.
Open I let the field recall its terrors of yester poem mind aware time.
Breathing is in and out of view seen through.

The poem sees the field seeing itself.
Is this a painting yet?
This story knows it is only story.

Free confessing I plagiarize our life together.
Side by side has singular syntax.
Sustainability is dialogical, well, omnilogical.

When it comes down to it I can't think of another time I'd rather be in, she said.
That we are accordingly in step is scarcely known in the fact of it.

Gap is not in itself a state of awareness.
We are the chosen nones.
The story about what's missing is truest when it ends.

Layers are what we don't know we're walking on.
This is one we're not picking up on.
If I knew its name why would I write on it?

Ordinary words are double agents for a future self.
The economy is if it's written something is happening.
We're on the verge of telling more than ever.

Profoundly the strays say.
For instance, I found my handwritten notebook left on vibrate by night.
I couldn't make this up if I tried.

The simplest thing is bottomless.
It's not happy if I can't read the curves fractually.
I stand commanded.

My personal part of speech just parted company.
Serial logic may well take note of what comes before and not much care.
If I show signs of acknowledging logically before *I* subject, I object.

I can't quite believe in serials except in the sense I know I'm being followed.
I'm on my hands and knees begging to be spoken through to.
Things don't mind going both ways at once half as much as you think.

Has it got that swing poetic?
Such impatient lives and yet the patient lives on.
No layering jives for long noetic.

Get swing.
In strange places, below this threshold, take wing.

Maybe you can't dance to it using your two legs but try the two sides of the brain.
Born of difference, refrain.

I thought I was trying to say something but it's not what it says.
It thinks all over and all along.

Omniverse is that for which we think at all.
The fat gut protects the small of the back.

Not all messages coming through are for me, it seems.
If I select I deflect.

You're never exactly in the river of time oozing past into future now, backflow so.
Exit alarms by the nature of out.

The deeper present likes no time.
It swings all the way down.

Readable time is passing you by.
Saving time, souls, dreams, minds, qi, not bankable.

Disbelieve everything that it have its fractal truth.
Listening to listening unpreconditions hearing.

A reference beams between the ears.

The thing said is gaining authority as we speak.
I find myself believing.
Obscurity rousing the faculties to act assures me I'm here right where I say.

It's all in the relationships you never can prove.
Spooky inactions right up close.
Paradox of an omniverse happy in its nature willing for the misery of just thinking.

Seeing things makes life is a dream business as usual.
Language stuffs. It has *no time* for you. The verb comes from behind.
Grammar is getting excited just when you think she isn't.

It's mind-degradable in that no matter the word orders break down.
Tracking wreaks. Turning transitives. Next thing you're a wreck deciding.
Logic beams inside frames including spherical waves.

This is where meaning comes in but no telling if it stays.
It minds.
Meaning is moody.

Deciding is not profundity itself.
Use is thinking through to the other end beginning now.
You can't measure the surround.

In principle you keep on track locus standi.
Breath registers the pull of the whole shaping now.
Unveil the lack a right to be heard.
And no way back.

Can't stop saying it's the tone timing burning through framed demonia.
You go to read and it's already falling face first.

Language frames in Klein perspective.
You don't go to read in the first place.

Pin me down I'm a butterfly.
Words aren't before they are.

Mind wormholes before calling it real.
Only the sideway slide lodges you off enough to hear over.

You catch yourself missing it.
Combines have no ends.

You go to speak and it's rising from the read.
The better dead is the one seen, coming.

Can't stop channeling the possible self.
Never not writing for the possible reader.

Take it from one created as you read.
Deciding real is reeling raw.

No one told you to.
Bend now so it unbinds before you.

I mean every word where every word means me.

It's not satisfying to think how I say it one nanosecond before.
People gather like sounding waters.
Flux wakes perfecting in what it flexes.

Finding a way to read it is never before.
Words have undercoating to come out only in some weather.
Sense is touch and go and feel in further.

Special opportunity is to get inside what you can't believe.
Other worlds look into your own opacity with unexperienced interest.
Tongue's opening to trickle-down politics of scarcely imaginable power figures.

If only we could keep it in verb.
Act inhabits its line projecting, housing.
Thoreau's map of the fields engraved in soul matter.

We cover the universe with drawings we have lived.
Mask is what speaks foremost never until now.
Being spoken to in through or before is daemonic already.

Its cause isn't.
Hearing homed.
Speculation mirrors.

She voices figure by me.
Texture is born shorn.
It's still not till feral.
No norm's not peril, born further.

21 *healing poetics*

Open space how much can fly ideas…
Pandit Pran Nath

You can't make noise.
To think it propagates a life.

Poem happily confirms understanding nothing.
Speaking true retracts identity for the duration.

Poetry like healing is an anomaly.
Its actual home is at the tip of the tail of a long-tail community.

A language you know is secret elsewhere.
Thinking dying dies in front of you.

Poetry heals when it heals poetics.
Nature in its actual mode of operation is anomalous.

Subjective unity is an impediment to internal diversity.
We lose track of who we are not judging.

Deep health is on the other side of hell.
How can it be the real me who dies?

When are we ever not judging? So who are we down here?
Death is the most extreme case of mistaken identity.

Healing begins in the ineptitude of expectation.
Deep health isn't sure which end is up and doesn't much care.

Healing is a state of inspired ignorance.

And you can't tickle yourself.
Indirection is one of the disguises of diversity.

We join apart in the distributive center.
I'm being quiet here, respecting heterogenesis of selves between us.

I must be dreaming neurodivergence of my proposed bodies—you're still here!
Indirect is the other kind of direct.

We're being induced as we speak.
I'm a late arrival but I'm taking up a lot of space, out of respect, loving the music.

Half the time I don't understand anything, and the other half I'm less sure.
Hands listen, body speaks.

Undertow under toe. Moves toward adding a categorial proprioceptive.
Things speak the way they are. *Resonant dissonance.*

I didn't come here to gather rosebuds, which are most everywhere like it or not.
While I may is while I say.

Raga sets the standard for serious waver.
It teaches behaving always other.

Sound leads, good deads, even more alive, thus said.
Deeds done under the sun are by definition new—what ever did they mean?

The long line of the law lies over self true news.

By indemnifying myself against the claims of the poem I make myself blameless.
Outside art it's a cheap trick.
No rabbits in this hole or even whole, no judges on this bench or present trench.

My Orphée mirror has worldly cracks and yet shows through to another side.
Talk straight and curve at large.
Weather decides.

There aren't enough straight lanes to double identity all the way.
The poem and its reading are not one, nor have we ever been.
Ordinary sincere voice convinces saying cockeyed things.

I hear your mind working overtime, she says over time to my reader.

What is called reading?
Ours not to compare but to do or dare, all too rarely.
Little doubt I'm losing it. And on another hand refusing it.

There's no only way by day.
Having your say at reading expense cuts in on the wrong dancer for good reason.
In heat or in bother is both ways at once.

World so harsh I'm so tired knowing I care.
Only satisfy doing.
Energy looses on its own swings.

We bridge by ridge.
True by tuning true.

The only thing that gets past doubt in linger mode is believable shock sense.
Listening hands lingering suck body parts partnering into the open.
The enemy cannot stay still or clear. This is all very technical.

No one reads all of anything. Nor all through and through.
Everything takes from somewhere appropriationally speaking.
Things next to each other take the conversation around the corner.

Does anyone actually think like oneself?
I scarcely catch half my meanings the first time round so what makes them mine?
No one likes everything about any other.

No one likes everything about oneself.
The order in which we think these things sets a rhythmic charge.
We're noting what can't be fully noted let alone notated in and of itself.

It takes two to wrangle. Well, one will do too.
The torque is in the take over and over.
This is no fandango unless you take it over.

Did anyone ask you to bring your own music?
You start the line as judge and end it as jury.
It's not a fandango without accompaniment. Technically.

I can only think what I think with what I know but the thinking's thinking more.
Speaking true is natural elegance in some of these cameos.

We jump to semi-conclusions and then on to the next flagrante.

True response is what could be, without saying when.
Figure coming to being with full force of origin figures forth fresh now the more.

Lingual learning goes poetic in altering your capacity to degrade by ripening.
"If you can't say something nice don't say anything" darkens.
Figuring primary is well versed summary execution.

I'm talking scenario sevens in search of an auteur.
The base struggle is to get your taut tongue taught.
Am I getting things backwards? Questions haunt and taunt. In no order.

Response is syntactic executive non-decision.
Construction implies induction followed by execution.

One can only follow so far until farther.
Any statement fails in the long run or else in curved runs.
What's hard is following between. Fun too.

I'm more distracted than anyone, just having to say this.
I get stranger everyday according to myself.
Looking in the mirror I see why revolutions fail.

What if I told you every line interns for absolute truth, differently.
Graduation is a limiting concept, whereas non-graduation unlimits ungradually.
Multiple negatives are positively negative.

Long-lived long lines occur like longing lives a letter at a time.
Self-assured criticism tells us we're who we want to be, at least for now.

I dreamt I was too unreal to wake up and face the greater unreality.
The container and the contained are in a death struggle or else a dance macabre.
I simply cannot tell you which is which in the present frame.

A poem is reading from which you derive being you no longer like they say.
The colloquial carries a heavy burden sounding true.
In truth the meanings are shooting stars.

The effort always is to give good sign.
The line disattends the reader letting a middle open way past.
The expression on her face is in my eyes.

Brightness falls in her lair.
I know she sees through my ecstatic singularity.

Questions bump the road under us.
Confidence is a function of its game.
The fall is in the familiar.

Don't come into my yard unless I say you can.
Yard poem goes with bird bard where mouth grew deep in the Deep South.
I fall into the familiar stepping on forbidden lines.

Pull the music from the thought and think to play it.
Are you sure you don't like it more when your ideology flies the kite?

The oracular spectacular lives… Exclamation punt.
I give up to keep the game live in confidence playing 'possum to fake out the dead!

I ask the unpreprocessing poem rising within me, *Think me!*
The mind knows the world filtered now refiltered to last.
A line retunes intelligence accordingly, tellingly.

I'm taking the easy way out without a question.
My question is how do I get all the way in.
Everything is saying itself true to itself in the eyes of the world.

No following the thought before it shows its truly false colors.
The question is how do we get traction when there's so much sliding about.
Question marks are not called for, and other remarks.

Skip commentary in the name of grammar.
May every word go front and center in time.
Why bother counting when the ragged raga's in the blood, alphabetically speaking.

Divine*d* revelation in the literal expression.
Letters dream words, lettered dreams word wyrder.
Excess of ordinary can glimmer prenormally.

It's not in your philosophy so don't bother looking.
Some thinking gets you by the balls, women not excepted.
Forget gender, lingual balls precede us.

It more gets you by the body than you think, should you think.
Taking offense gets you off the hook.
Learn them letters to integrate, said Sparky.
Please take it wrong, it's our only hope of getting along going off the road.

This is turning into a personal conversation between us remaining nameless.
The poem tests a hypothesis you haven't yet arrived at.
We're talking good economy with prethinking, thinking, postthinking simultaneous.

Born of a common flaw never the same.
Hopeful at the end of our feather.
Takes no smarts to listen smart, thankfully.

The sublime subliminal is liminal to any proposition and so necessary hereabouts.
It could never get us to think its way other than wisely advisedly.
The art of falling through the sentence, glossobatic, survival-syntactic, catch me!

Weird word *wyrd* shining through's crazy, ask anyone.
It's like roots talk turnkey subinverted narratives of personal origin, *me word!*
If you deny haunting poem say you lie like Chinese ancient calligraphy, no hands.

This is where you let the dragon ride you.
It's a figure of speech with wyrd wings.
You let it out of its cage it lifts you out of yours.

What's so mystical about fruitcake truth taking you for a ride beyond.
No question mark has ever been more visibly invisible.
We come together to hide the better to get some free space miraculously.

Remember nothing meaning the same would dare show its face here.
Nevertheless it makes its presence felt in the slide between senses.
That's that verbal tickle that that dragon that flew through pooh-poohed, aslant.

pronominal reflex

My poem arrives too late to find meaning.
Longlasting ideas must be poetically inexperienced.
The poem remains by fiat for the time of its spark.

You know the affection is real when it's never ideal.
If only this were memorable it would weather the failings of memory, briefly.
Rereading the lines long enough switches to mental circular breathing.

Serial telling requites serial living.
When multiple readings are real one isn't true unless all are.
Interpretation interrupts innuendo on and on.

Quit your twitching, quips the bird word.
Penis is the original buzz word that coming upon makes you buzz.
Time castration and its opposite timely castration suffer us the logic of buzz.

When I notice my mind it speaks and this is what it sounds as.
A line is level on squeezed-in leveling watch.
Vagina is the original buzz word that coming upon makes you fuzzy.

Obviously you is flexible engendering.
Repurpose purpose one pronoun at a time many a time.
Stopping here leaves us only with poem as we know it.

The possible reader is smarter that her maker.
Rely only upon a no fit situation.
The world is on loan from language.

...when you cut word lines the future leaks out...
William Burroughs

Today I'm in rehearsal for being a possible me.
One is a collection.
There's nothing waiting here in the back of this vehicle.

Attitude's fundamentalism's feeling's believing.
Clearly my detractors keep me honest, even when I'm not sure they bother to exist.
True tone sequesters between emphatics: *Honestly they make me up this way.*

I can't shake the sensation of attitude swirl.
It looks like openness but it feels like torque.
There's a twist in the chassis grammatically speaking.

There's no poetry, there's scarcely poets.
Thinking it makes me feel trapped in a category error.
Happily outed dogmas become minddegradable.

The status is clearest when least bearable.
My internal vehicle frame holds up an artificial object in its construction plus words.
You know it's poetic when the next morning it destabilizes the maker.

Poet humility crafts identity primping.
Poetics as self study in a lingual mirror as as is is.
Acknowledged dogma's less dangerous becoming minddegradable in the voice.

Poetry is disagreeable.
In a world of singularity statements rust out rapidly.
Some unsettling issues never settle down.

31 *post-grammatical rolling chassis*

Thinking deeply wants to say mind is scale invariable, and then she shows up.
No one thinking stays and when I distract or detrack it still waves landscape rhythm.
Nothing gets said but it alienates gendering.

Double dealing pools to say here.
We're being framed as we speak.
Still my valences are running wild.

The gramma of all anima projections is laying out the filters.
We may never get the straight story on fax sex, but narrative isn't everything.
The voice owns every poetic event ever heard and this is feedback.

Surface is sex waiting to happen.
My anima was last seen in Iceland trekking the eponymous ice.
The self enjoys no end to her vexation.

Holding back from limiting is limiting further than.
Narrative fields feel forth her here.
A poetry of opposition faces the fixity of source, and then she walks in while out.

Put your paten where your poem's at in memory of her standing there now.
Time is folding the tent as we speak.
Poetry proves anomalous if anyone is wondering.

No problem with subject and object both ways like we do.
If there's a break it's I'm changing hands.
We do this because it's required by the nature of knowing it is.

Ladies, gentlemen, children, pets, semblables, we're here to talk past each other.
If you think it you did so feel free to keep right on.
Wish youse were here.

In the middle of the voice is the middle voice in potentia.
That the speaking forfend upending our medial many.
Talk down to it till it talks itself up.

It can take all night to get to the point where listening gets through barely.
Crack of dawn, lack of scorn, life forlorn. Torn vowels.
Bene, bene, my valences are streaming wild.

It's now and always will be.
Poetics is self study where self is distributed as studied.
This is unauthorized by its claim to be at the heart of the poem.

This reminds me a poem has the advantage of not knowing what it thinks.
No need to constrain focusing listening.
The concept is on the way.

The form is what eyes you back satisfactorily.
At least one of youse has to agree.

The once and future now is sacred like a cow.
Lies are emptiness; emptiness is a lie.
This is as true as it gets in a fit.

I vowed to remain calm when I saw myselves inseparable from the eye of the storm.

We're here to get back to where we are.

I voweled to not get here before you and failed self exceeding.

The truth makes no claim to be true.

I can't think how hyperactive my unconscious must be today to get me this out.

The poem outs by way of ins.

Nature balances in the absence of balance to stay.

Undertime slacklines our view thanks to the quicksand timing of the text.

She offers a hand for no pulling up.

The once and ever non efforts naturing.

Poetry's intel on unknown intelligent non sense.

Consonance in consonants concerns no one unto time untold.

Order waters the implants.

Thinking doesn't know it counters intelligence until the intel is in.

I'm getting greener.

One day I'll talk in tala teental till the cows come tale in tow.

You may ask why you make me cry.

The answer is some things may be said to be trying.

And some things try not.

Makes for three.

You will see.

34 *coming in twos and off the handle*

dha dhin dhin dha| *dha dhin dhin dha*|
dha teen teen ta | *ta dhin dhin dha*|

The teaching is a new way to read like it or not. Listen over.
Keep trying till you hear your both at once.

Telling your story stops it telling you you.
Stop telling in time to be told.

Doppelganger's just mirror text talking back.
Don't take it personally lest you not take it at all.

It's just saying I have nothing to say about it.
Tell me when it tells you too.

Thing is you can't tell being addressed as a letter like you are.
Postage due is you do.

Don't expect a tale to wag like god tongue or dog sung.
It's off the hook the moment you look.

Deal is you get out of your hatch.
Now comes the part about no itch to scratch when you lift the latch.

We can go on like this because like this you go on.
Sounding silly gets your other attention to learn retention.

Single sensation's sensational intention.
Going from two to three is to an other be.
By the law of flaw you flay but it gets you to say you are, loretorn.

waking from myself

for Raquel Rabinovich

My life rhythms are off today and I'm slipping into tell it like it is mode.
No guarantees with syntactic reassurance and zero point insurance.
However life and death no two frames are an exact match.

You have to cross a double line to go both ways at once.
Physicists claim to understand how this works, I do not.
Reality is the greatest bad metaphor ever.

How many hurt spots in body, in mind show up in microscopic tonal view today?
Everything appears unreal like the poem and so it matters more than we *think*.
Happy thinking it's not me thinking, it's mind in its nature, which does not think.

How many *its* does it take to make a fit fit?
If it's loaded and promises firepower enough to kill me, I'll imagine it for starters.
Maybe it's enlightened registering the scale-invariable rhythms beginning to end.

Everything is sinking into the background so it must be time.
Or else ecoproprioception is finally kicking in and I'm sensing my self as this field.
I is as many as I and we are alone here.

A sentence is a field where my first question is how it plays me in its way.
I forget the beginning by the end and throughout the middle variously I see it.
Part of the conceptual frame here is the promise to find out my intending *on*.

Cards on the table the deck complete or not.
Self-knowing is a card at a time and may never make it to inline number.
And not one think at a time thinks itself necessary here.

2 *testing the hypothesis you can't dance at all the weddings*

I am being given, if may venture the expression, birth into breath.
Being proprioceptively right takes nothing away from anyone leaving no self behind.
Illness is not the devil but the ball bouncing back.

Going wrong evolves.
I'm a loser winning big like never.
Looking so far down now no past appears.

Heart breaks too easily to stand too easily public.
Here we are surviving our mismatched frames.
I lie on another who lies well under.

The title entitles and the poem goes dancing.
Too close body reading performs hypochondriacally generic.
A poem embodies playing out things calling it into question.

What is the principle of the moment if not momentous momentum à point.
Here's the sole locus dance points to.
Definition is never dead-on, so what's the point of dying over words?

The order is far too complex to believe.
It's what speaks to you that hears you.
It's a poem when the word can make you gag.

My vocabulary is out of control still doing this to me.
Have you met my wife, glossia, said the lexicon in charge.
Her mission's to get us to say what language *is* by going with where it's never been.
This is not an allegory nor *read only*.

My dogma is I don't believe in dogma.
I'm convinced there's an actual entity *poetry* if only that it won't not address.
Safe with one where safety last lasts.

Include me out at the end of the day unendingly.
Certain matters are not in our hands and the tongue could care less suspendingly.
Apprehension is underrated.

My autobiographies arising in counterpoint stir the blot on character(s).
Slips of the rung make space for the truly unsung.
Neither hung up nor strung up is retention.

Nesting art has a manner undisclosed.
It tests the hypothesis what it says is unknown to us according with our capacity.
Implied is a species of life saying live in its own sense.

Pressing down on life mysteries gets a rise out of being in Easter mode.
Story is a provocation to the capacity of belief.
Bringing it into the body here splits it down the middle, and now we're middling.

Can one bear the intensity of getting to the linear end staying sharp?
Don't answer so quick.
Put some drag on mind.

Get some lag time just in time.
Shine the gap, light sky mind.
Slogans are welcome in hell.
Let us go then you and I in our diamond sky where rhyme dies hard.

Self heresy saves souls.
Like Faust one thing does not lead to another as thought.

Proprioceptive poiesis writes in my dark.
Read slowly as fast as possible.

But I don't have to tell *you* this if as it seems you're actually here.
No there there but plenty here.

Poetry is the more you don't dare say.
Putting our work under threat outs the inadmissible evidence against us.

The daimon of poetry fucks with your mind in uncertain terms.
Failing better and better is not just a literary option.

Every excursion of mind is a digression from the unaccounted center.
All necessary for spirals to redeem.

You can call this *intervention in blank space* but will it come?
I approach these matters with proprioceptive blind faith/seeing in the dark.

The mirror does well to select never.
The rearview goes ever before.

Feeling good in the face of death is the whole point in pointless space.
Look mom no lands.

Any according discovery blocks unaligned undiscovereds.

I was walking along speaking my own sound no one heard including me.
A thinking has a music thought knows not.

Never select is a mirror motto.

You can't help happening in no time round.
Never catch the mind on the way to the bottom where it starts.
Can never find ear stumblers till way too late.

Lineal proprioception knows from the start when the end is nigh.
No balance in nature but that going in and out.
At one sharpening point can you think it.

See what your friends are saying. Find friends. Can't miss these instructions.
Staying ahead of the game is not playing.

A war against the self turns against the body.

It's rough here, hands running over all and out.
You can define it but it's not definitive.
What is most alarming is that it's still not hearing in return. To arms!

The near singer cultivates her insanity to sing.
It keeps coming back so you wonder aloud.
At the wave crest what is thinking but transfinity?

The way in is through the back door, why is it no one will use this method.
Her song too wise to not make crazy.

Time to cultivate inner noise.
Sharp waves in dark shark caves and bones to cover.

My scholar's mind can't help cheating on beauty.

What is thinking but it calls itself back?
Stepping tones to heaven gone dark.
Light my spire. I feel it in my elite feet knowing to place.

Truth cracking is an acquired taste.

What is singing but it calls itself out?
Following the rules makes up rules on the go.

A great statement hunts down its objects.
There are no exact equivalents.
The notion of equivalence is not exact anymore ever *ever*.

Language goes off on its own when you're not fixed right on it, if I can say this.

Numbers also break under their own weight reaching the lips.
As soon as body gets into it counting torques.

You can feel it like the ear on its knees.
Thought has breeze.

The self-true referent falls between.
Pairs think accordingly.

7

Hear past.

I don't remember writing this.
Self-persistence in denial is raging from behind.
The line is a pick-me-up thrown out over to here.

My palette of beliefs is blood spatter resurfacing.
This is not on the level but optimal full tilt.

A line is an only memory.
Next is less only.

It's never as easy as it fails to seem.
Half way through it feels like a cam model with no watchers.

The pervasive music is sub-audible in undertime.
No pretending to repeat.

You can't say straight what won't straighten.
Actual open is middle distinction discrimination.

Spread leg eyes see what sees.
Secrets aren't buried but burrowing.

Lofting intensity suffers unending completion.
Skewed sense is a sign of arrival midair.

Tune is airborne.

Imagine singing bodies thinking music making body.

Living as if eternal recalls eternity well under escaping mind.
You say what you don't know you're saying but know it knows what it says.

I know I'm here to solve first dissolving.
It's talking in me cross lingual membranes so silly expecting to understand.

Poetry is the holdback medium leaving space for undiscovering, truth (un)folding.
The retaining image goes unseen until it flashes in your mind further along.

There is sound health unknown.
It has undertiming.

Thinking addressing someone exercises representing known thinking.
The voice a thing is said in finds the open space so resonant, or fails to.

Meditating on thought necessarily self-meditates.
The poem is irritating beauty.

Noise is unheard music.
Don't play it again, Sam.

Being who was born is optional.
What is life force but the same well always.
No wonder we think like this but yes wonder.

---

2 *in memorium Kishori Amonkar (10 April 1932–3 April 2017)*

9

noise talk

. . . leave some heaven behind. . .
Sonny Rollins on Coltrane

My cellular fireflies flick out without me.
Today I hope to catch up with my body.

Solve the thought and coagulate the syntax.
Getting through any line disrupts to serve up in the end before getting there.

Thinking gets confused looking through itself, may it find another way.
Sway [imperative].

The half ununderstood phrase jolts the mind to seek out the unimagined.
How judge while the daily rereading is the same never again reading?

How we pace, which foot electing to stay behind, which hand enowning.
Root in place unstoppably all along.

Reading seeds.
True as verbality with its singular coherence figuring itself out further ongoing.

The whole doesn't stop for the part.
The part proposes a poetics that doesn't belong whole sail.

The matrix mothers the bastard word moving center out.
False etymologies root more logically than true.

What's the point of pointing but to attract lightning.
Light fire.
Firelight [*transperative*].

I'm just now out speaking the day's vibeweb.
The body is wiredly narrative.

It speaks an unlike music.

Sound ideas mind image.
Cello infracts waking tone, barrel frictive.

The poem depends on the reader to give it its scant sense of meaning.
It fails to please as it falls to ecstase.

No vacation, it's as vacant as it gets.

Falling apart creates its own verb beside itself with meaning.
Intelligence oozes between syllables.
Stake your heart claim letting blood talk.

Our collective is tracking events across their verbal webwork.
Here we have certain signals with uncertain weights.

We know who we are *doing*.
Bump back to jumpstart the verb cut off.
Suprasegmentalia genitalia generate genetically, just saying.

Traduction if you open your mouth.

You tap the feeling for energy enough to send a rocket, or settle for thinking it.
There's no not stepping with imaging webbed foot.

Slowly I seem to be waking from the dream of myself.
Soon I will break the fast pacing to nourish.

Healing is self healing, creation is self creation.
The poem I love rejects my explanation.

Double the flow to trouble the show.
You know you have legs walking, ideas talking.

The real body you never see talks before you ever hear.

Mind is happening before brain.
Body is ideational, imaged.
My shopping list body walks its talks.

What's the rush? is a poetics inquiry.
Mind impresses body.
The time it takes remains untaken.

It sounds fixed and it's not political in that sense.
It suprasegments touching.
It makes an impression to be itself.

Just press. Nothing to express. Fail to digress.
It's not patience to meet all the parts needed but living duty let loose.
Wide awake eyes gaze wide.

Scripture on water never ceases writing itself.

12 *mind finds mine*

The body is a blind mouth sucking existence.
William S. Wilson

Belief of the moment rules worlds.

We're swinging between thinking pattern and less than that, other sensing.
I'm not as smart as I think I'm not.

Body feeds back to better feed forward or possibly around.
Just ask it—it takes two—souls, or any number greater than one.
It's likewise important to acknowledge your participation in collective deformation.

Get real reading knows it's approximate and probably confused.
Gift the world a righteous sense of chaotic balance.
Falling summons powers.

Poetry's hunt for reliable articulatory force bogs down under rule stress.
It inspires the idea of itself.

Being fully where you are takes no notice of unscruteworthy sequence.
Invention of what you don't have summons a shaping force.

Words deform by emotional force.
I feel my brain trying to catch up with my mind.

Body knows the world as itself and itself as the world.
The world finds its nose in the dark as I find mine, you wish.

Environment is a talkback feelback affair.
News that was not before said.

Are sounds I'm making laughter or anguished cries or else music from far within?

Lingualities retain forces in their own ways.
What I mean for it to be saying is what it's telling me it holds back.
Mind tricks itself which is why we let there be syntax trickery for self-protection.

Poem has a message poet knows not.
Writer goes elsewhere and the poem comes here.
Not I am here to tell you even as I tell myself not.

Sense is born not made.

Apologies for getting personal which is never as easy as it seems.
Don't do nothing as nothing does.
Mind knows strong in the music.

Mind eyes co-orientation lets you see what it sees through selfsame eyes.
The difficulty here is self undoing pattern.

A singularity doesn't know it's special.
Resolve nothing.

No line once but calls twice minimal. [*reroute on*]
Next meaning is bounceback in that hall calling itself inner.

Resolution's dissolution.

Slogans bond bogus armorial memorials.

It's all so lifelike and lineally cleansing.

Must be a lab for recombinant thinking.

I can't help mumbling to you from across the room and other vast spaces.
Every space meant verbally toned dumdumdum sounds syntactic antic yet sublimes.

Apologies for getting impersonal which is never as difficult as you'd like.
There's only one surface and one temporality proving one is not quite a number.

The appropriational goal stresses live function to the bone.
Wait till I get my hands on your poetics and tone.
I abuse the term you.

I'm stepping over the preferred pronoun impeding the straight and narrow.
Still feeling our time here squeezed.
We are not holding hands between words.

The loneliness of the long-distance meaner, her many swerves.
Not patience but holding the curve right along.
Swing time timing.

You are not folding bonded word betweens until you really are.
Sounds do not so much mean as dream toning no beginning before now.
What you hear is who you are.

We are nanoseconds athwart.
We part before thinking meaning reading.
Just sinking in is not a matter of duration.

No playing it again, Sam, ever.
Music runs on never running out.

The actual personal is singular.
Truth is unreliable.

Singing is fire in the eyes.
Meaning at a distance is.

Blake sees you seeing Blake.
Amita Sinha sees you singing through her.

Seeing itself sees what it can't.
Provisional thinking is its own provision.

Truth is burning before your eyes.
Scripture is text no one dares want to write.

Aswing between base and fine sings on the wing.
I never quite understand the lyrics.

Am I even real off this line?
What refuses to hook you never lets you off the hook.

You sense the subsyntactic raga sideswipes the poem thinking.
What you read is not on the page but falling between the elements of focus.

It gets physical like it or not you like it.
A flash in the pan between life and death is beating out the sentence.

Joyous metaphor sprints as two-way carries a one-way force.

Sometimes walking past a thing I glimpse its aim to be itself startling.
A week day has aroma at a distance at any distance.
This is the narrative resisting narrative almost successfully.

It wants work, it lacks what it makes, it transfuses its trance for entrance.
Talking drums in messages until tracking hearing hears back.
How many whirls in the ear of a pen.

I couldn't get at the idea in my hip until it stammered.
Wyrd senses in whorls.
Walking passed a thing mumbling.

Recording is not for future hearing but to physically reflect.
Interlacing impacts make tracks.

She teaches, call her Emily, collaboration with death (life knows to be).

Hating losing holds me away.
How are we apart in such a place.

It flows you forward in lineal flower force.
Tumbling on, assembling lorn and passing.

Welcome to her labyrinth moving on.
It sounds secret as I sound the horn interlinear.
The sole trap sets at reading behest.

When I look back I see myself looking forward to now.

Time to track mistepped leaks into the future.

True oppositions tap their separating wall calling worlds to weave.
Verbals separate to link. Space rime.

The actual personal singular grammaticizes no one willing.
Hating proverbs pays dividends in pointless space.

What soul is is what heals here, saying is.
The green force fuses the words that say it and can't.

What passes through sees through.
Verse reverses without saying versus.

The poem teaches happiness retention crossing the abyss.
Or say climbing the mountain in progress in the eye of the endless storm.

This is the place where anything is said and unsaid with equal unknown meaning.
Satisfaction guaranteed unrecognizable.

Hover craft meaning.
The lift is on the spot.

Skillful beans. Speaking inside skulls. Refleshing freshly.
Carrying my own weight with no hands to show for it.

The reader is never asked to know her own mind, not one nano instant too soon.
For the text part scriptured on the curve is thinking before you know it.

Without even noticing it you change your tone.
Just when you thought it'd gone bone dry.
This place did not develop nor was it born this way.

Sooner or later everything made self grammaticizes.
Self regeneration codes genie in the bottle.
Here I am at another wit's end over the tip of the tongue claiming unbeknownst.

Just because I can't prove its grammar doesn't mean I'm not held in.
Meaning teaches vertical.
It's piled just so high. Quality of air.

No name can say who's present in her lines.
Listening is itself before you can hear.
The aim is to be receptive to what is asked for receiving.

Medium is what takes you in focusing on inkbodied words living it up.
I'm the prisoner of verbal charm soulsaking animation.
Its gravitas is a killer. Sin tax.

Darkness falls from her stare.
I'm making this up heading off her making me up even more.
Text is neutral on gender making space for distinguishing marks.

Rime signals same indifferently self-altering never again now.
The nail hits itself on the head in a curving dimension.

For the poem can't resist scripturing on a curve to think before you know it.

19 *the afore mentioned soul saving self heresy*

I fear we're not getting rid of God
because we still believe in grammar.
Nietzsche

How many times do I need to say what has yet to be but can't quite?
This aims to take to an edge the fact language makes no promise to communicate.
Even high sincerity appropriation is on the take.

Trying not to try to think thinks far too much.
What is yet to be is what you can take in starting now.
Poetry proves soul works for a living.

The taste a line starts from is not the same as end of line tasting.
A line draws itself out till cutting off.
A reader cuts out at the start of interpreting.

Temporarily going visually deaf finds a way unfounded.
The choice happens about midway in the voice.
Minding is roundabout either way and both.

Just saw the middle that isn't there.
Taking it all the way in is never far enough.
Happiness retained cannot be contained.

Seeing through blind mys miming minding.
Factually speaking blue whales rime—out of the blue.
Phyllotactic spirals whorl syntactic true.

Do plants know they speak mind? is rhetorical.
Language traps wild willing in a lingual bee yard.

unvoiced middle

Without contraries is no evolution.
Ontononymous the Particular

What holds mind held high suspended in clear space?
Don't try to answer that until well aloft.
The art is hanging back while leaping over, keeping one ever.

We've been here forever in the middle, such is the parabolic natura between.
Forever is the partner of eternity living apart within oneselves.
The disease of context sheds hard.

The text picks it up and packs it back in.
Everything is saying more than it knows.
Everything is here where you put it.

It's the lilt in the letters in the voice on the page.
Little 'lectrics lecturing us all falling.
Tall tale laid low, saying more than it shows.

I show up to myself tale first.
I incarnate naming narrativizing.
If I say I it's to remind myself I can regardless.

I is writing in the sand.
Whales rhyme accordingly.
Conscious contraries know where they're going never having been.

Thinking like wind blown knowing.
We can only say things thinking themselves.
Middling possibly feels like thrown through. Suspense.

Romantics are hiding in multiple kinds of logic, and most joyous are paraconsistent.
There's no avoiding sliding down thinking axis. Thrill!
Just by opening your mouth truth empties out with no need in speaking.

A tiny letter tears through hoping.
This type of hole strikes through, true.

If you can think it it means it.
Not soulful, soul pull.
It's how it holds you here.

It shows by itself as by another.
Speaking is no matter what weighing on.

We be bees pressing our kind in time.
Not evil, error.

Ideas kick around with unrecognizable drive alive otherwise.
It's how you hear it holds you here and there.
No fear errs shaking out.

Choosing to move on the spot renders precise respite.
Language is thinking on its inside serve.
We swerve to go head on.

She talks flight in hearing blight, she has her way with mind.
The logics paraconsist, two legs getting to town and no frown.
Swan swing.

22 *fire rises above desperation*

We are the last first readers.
Ontononymous the Particular

Loving history is our vie for durable significance.
Religiously I believe in orthography. At least so far this near.
If the last, we can last.

The curve of the phrase induces the phase modulating energy.
The sentence is to not know a moment before—or after for that matter.
Everything happens by the syllable.

I dream, therefore I'm not.
The poem proves proving erotic in the curve.
The body is absolute here.

A gift of gravity is non-analgesic poiesis.
Self-knowing afield wakes in bodied politics.
The music is playing together surfacing curve.

Either/or's on the head of a pin matters not how many.
Directed is without direction.
Finding the vocal gaps keys many manners.

Cherished thoughts repel enemy thoughts feeling their oats.
The dead I'm dreaming verge live to dine with us.
Old time feels lost still complaining.

Aswim in the grand continuum canyoning the hole surrounds the line.
Tense timing holds on in.
The music is the spring in the trap toward home.

Welcome to the town that wasn't here until you arrived.
Friendly starts in the home grown out. Out still here.
Linguality doesn't get its power from the thing.

The past is listening in on the present, poetically bespeaking.
Only just arriving opens the hole wider yet, and yet.
Fire rises without going toward.

Never by the book but under.
The singer burns, up.
Mirror neurons reach out self claiming.

Another way of saying this is still born to come.
A poem is remembering its body on the way.
Time minds swinging back on itself, to be said.

The line starts so to be what it isn't by the end.
The raga is still staying, saying other.
Rhythm runes a matter hands free.

Poem is ever only just passing through.
Verb steeds full force fusing ahead.
Writing however tricky is never the equal of mind.

You feel the pull into the perplex you mirror.
Orphée morphs olé duende.
Line aggression is birth all over.

I'm getting ahead of myself thinking back to the beginning of thinking this.
I come this way doubting I ever did, turns out it's right.

I still don't know its means to know what means. Or if. Even if.
Language doesn't tell you it thinks in shapes.
It knows it's tricking like a bad knee streetwise.

My suppression is worth still going under. Pulse is up.
Message is the language listening to what it knows.
Hope is everything I say will be taken another way, even by me.

In the biological mirror the killer is killed.
Right reading is when the poem reveals we're in sync.

If you look carefully Orphée is gloved piercing liquid mirror mercury.

Everything said happens back here another way.
The line can't help enacting my aggressive tendency to be born.
Throwing out now the idea of place, catch.

We keep pushing at each other as the rug pulls out.
This book is exactly like all the others letting themselves go.
This is the catch, it catches on itself, going uncaught.

Deluging negative thoughts are clearing out, Orphée.
The music is showing the inside how lighting bears, bares.
The sun is coming out today—with a vengeance.

Negative thoughts about negative thoughts about negative thoughts running out.

This is how I know what's real to the point of satisfaction.

We run rugged syllabics over rough stuff.
Feeding on the music out in the wilder wild.
Flow is the stream I manage to get up into right above hereunder.

Invariance is the part about handling itself bewaved.
A music's where it hears itself through cracks and harsh havens.
This keeps coming back as the earth's births aren't flat lacks.

Syntax leaks. Suddenly you hear snakes and their ragas.
Art does not cover life.
Your life minded resurfaces.

The poem doesn't say where I am, so no sense longing for elsewheres.
I'm locating quantum entanglements by foot.
Measure levels your arrivals.

Walking to & fro takes time going down tripping, tricked over, obstacular.
And did those feet in ancient time is a question to come.

Reread I love you that rewrite is not over you.
Wanting to believe in images true as a voice—personando.
Fiction is problematic for an imagination literalist—true reliever.

Competing versions suffer the same rut.
I'm going inside where it lets you walk to & fro.

Where it's happening is prime mystery and time again keeping an eye on eternity.

We don't have to weigh the future in any line, the given, the weighted.

Whatever can be thought there takes place in its place.

Weighting words in place of waiting. Time and again.

This is a moment of irresistible hovering in verbal wild.

It's only the sound in its position.

Self shaping over taking.

Whatever can be felt shaping biophones that you hear unnaming.

Sidewinding ecstasy takes chances that aren't.

Don't bother understanding. [sign on the road to verbal paradise]

What have you even done for me lately, still happening and far from sense.

It won't hold because it doesn't.

The life verb overs its edge.

The sun is hiding, tired of war.

Writer's block is identity cramp inside war camp.

Competing ruts, rutting down.

No excels falling down wells, self spills spells.

Reread *I tell you.*

Imagining literally, self spells.

Raga talking itself up moves toward an ending everywhere hands still on.

27 *the music creates the instrument*

Existence perfects self-exclusion
Ontononymous the Particular

Anything is plausible in a world that thinks fungible.

A line never tells you what to do.
Not to determine what comes next but to receive in the clear.
Syntactically speaking, and not only.

If I said it once I've said it thrice greater: *NO SAME LINES.*
Verbal fractals actually.
No! same lines, fr'actually.

Pen point scratches page itch, and there is word.
If everything were true, and it is, the world would exceed itself, unlimited undoing.
Now for the theory of the throughcomposed life.

Life line. I mean the poem only (ever) happening life on the line.
Its verb has swivel verve, flesh-stripping strength.
It can't let itself go down easy.

How you take it in depends on being taken in, refugee, the fool.
Music and instrument, chicken and egg, nesting.
Narrative rushes the issue forth. Stop.

To divine own mind be through.
Scale is variable according to state of mind and grammar supposed.
No line sits comfortably.

Mind fit scales.
When every step goes earth center you've landed.

Conscious life proceeds from misunderstanding.

Feeling free's not just any spree.

You let it speak when it thinks you're ready.

Lacking composure gives the throughgenerating life.

It keeps secrets from itself for safety sake.

Inside eating. Fleet. Bird keeping the sky inside.

It's hard to break the habit of understanding everything.

There's a phone ringing in the next life, not for me.

Understanding nothing is impossible.

Stop that preferring before it drags you down under seeing level.

Proud conscious eludes the joy self sustaining.

Eventually meaning one thing after another pop pop pop. Stop.

Keep some philosophic static in the line to birth its unheard music.

The phone ringing in a past life thinks it's still for me.

The trouble is not believing in the inevitable magic incursion.

Mother is home STOP okay to question source STOP help to follow

It comes down to being heard.
Message a matter of primacy deferred.

Promises to keep before sleep on the road forsaken in the promised sand.

Our land slides to be ours.

The poetic estate knowing has no business being real.

Life and art mirror mirror on the soul.
If there were sides *which one would you be on?* is a mirror question.

Poetry can't help fueling aggressive ideas.
In my unwritten poem I am rushing around looking for being in the next room.

Even dark thought takes cover from unspoken elegance.
Pull it up to your ears letting eyes through.
The clock numbers keep signifying *regardless*, except now.

It's being drawn into a complexity you mirror. By alterity.
Then there's walking through, each step.
Emphasis on being speaks the lingual mirrored more.

The animal lives in that we sniff every corner.
The music hears through the veil without getting caught up veiling.
Plucking spectator sport strings still it sings curved.

Landing cites.
Music eyes.
Ditto means it still isn't.

The distal idea is ever in the middle half-formed, half trying to get away.
My brain state is hiding from me right here, can't you feel it?
It's hard to grasp this matter hands free.

I speak tree when no one is looking including me.
This is how you know the mind works further behind your back.

Where you end up is not all of you.
You're still echoing the still unborn note.

Lines ride you. Mosquitoes ride raindrops.
Being is approached approaching.

Not to forget the forgetting.
Smoke blackens rising.

Keeping the faith requires a waiver.
True stepping no stopping and less stooping.

All words are last words.
How else the inscription on the underbelly of the great unreality.

He thinks before he thinks and therefore he is before he is.
Words in their nature are first words age whatever.

Old art repealing time is new art revealing mind.
My life a single breath.

Poem implores reader not to become a trapped animal.
Real punishment is before the act and timely.

We lose time all the time.
When the flow stops I stop.

What you want to hear is never already there yet always unhearing.

Slinking through mind forest this means leaking your perspective, quick.
Tripping through the day as never usual.

Tales from the glyph cliff. Sounds clutch. Voice crimps.
Message from afar, across the page, room, living.

Like music it never leaves the body behind and never leaves the body. Ever.
Last words are first words mirroring the words to come.

(Un)channeling is where she says and unsays at once and you write and unwrite.
Reading erases as it goes it shows.

A purpose of poetry is to see beyond purpose as in the mirror darkly.
Glass syntax, quicksilver semes.

We can't imagine an alternate dimension and then we do. But not quite again.
Coming is coming across and over. And over.

An absolute event in whole-mind reading. *Dead sing slant.*
Played space for the dead to roam and learn to dream us back. Do over.

There are endless new ways to get here and still not know what we're doing.
There's the mirror for never again.

We're warming up to them and this is the heat on.
Twist it with the right touch and ghost mirrors.

Believe the image not itself believing.

Let me clearly not claim.
Poem subtractively clamors.
Sender genders by decree. I listen.

Poetry is an intention getter.
It knows what it's doing even more than I say.
Claiming is believing.

Gender decides to be on a sliding scale.
When I leap out of this body may her poetics lead the way.
No names please. I'm enjoying the vivid calm.

Reading here is a certain movement around excited syllables.
The door reads no (en)trance between walkings through two-ways at once.
A kind of slide altering as it goes under and on.

I am the message leaping across nerve cells of the selving polydimensional structing.
A statement feels its own curve following embedded passions now surfacing.
Names pleasure regardless.

Poetry is an attention loser finders keepers.
Gender likewise knows itself on a curve.
I am being spoken accordingly.

My animism is still studying.
It's not not not happening—I'm losing track.
Rightness right here.

It's your art when you know it takes a lifetime. Maybe more.
Likewise reading entangles poem.

There's a certain nervousness to the purpose self-seeing on a curve.
Poem spaces believing free in free fall.

It finds more than existing.
It progresses still at every moment.

Poetic seriousness requires not being taken seriously as you do.
Comfort zones fester quick.

Dreams relieve a need for more here here.
All views are extreme when you get right down on it.

The single note extends longer than you think.
Literal ally offers its virtual alley.
Skipped personality flips personally.

The view grows stronger by way of its contrary.
Field sentience makes sense.

Accordance at a distance is spooky live.
We're a house know away and a tone's show saying.

Word loans land lone as they may.
Poem disagrees with you for you.
Once two hands know themselves separate they can know together starting out.

34 *mirror turn ons*

I'm the medium for the music.
Anupama Bhagwat

Body art embodies the art as own body.
And build a life thereon upon and on and on.
You are the surface of your waking dream and double. Now triple.

By what direction I am feeling sentient speaking cannot tell itself.
Links drop.
Lines take pains to flare intercellular.

Looking everywhere an affect for a reason effects.
Vertical writing's looking through you letter by letter.
Rhythm is taking you by remise.

The agen blight infit meaning you go by what goes.
You half turn back to walk straight curving, heel heals.
Accumulates where you've stopped looking.

Miraculous misery only ever leaks.
Ideas mind image ahead stepping on over.
I feel a tracker among leakers.

Hearing calling from afar hears itself still coming.
It's the poem with belly smarts.
It's seeing the date of very far along and still reaching over.

Vertical and horizontal at once the music is ending never yet knowing what it is.
Sing along then. Voice plus.
And yet it knew everything all along you would never believe.

non binding horizon

for Mikhail Horowitz

1 *just doing*

I can't die.
Blanchot

Why leave traces? Don't answer that.
We will never get back to this place.
Here waits for no one.

I'm moving on from my bath of pale fire.

Life and death can't stay away from each other.
There's no substitute for daily dying.
Fulfilled in the rip further fills by rip.

We're always one step ahead where life is yet to arrive.
This is where I see myself in the mirror differing and letting be differing.

Haunting happens before line ends. Like lineage.

A god is what you make up as you are made up.
Exploiting difference locates sameness even as it fades.
The system does not show where it will show up—just that it will.

The point you miss is behind your clouds.

That you think my poem before me makes it mine in fire.
Reading indirection mirrors writing self-direction.

Poetry is about not interfering with how it sits on the page or hangs in the air.
Life too. And the unending haunted betweens.

I am born mirroring.

If we don't know how we got here how is there a where to?
Clearly I am what I am yet to discern.

How is it never over as you know.
Now doesn't admit it's ever not.
The message of a work is its doing. You mirror further.

Where is the end in sight as if I could hear it?
My priorities are turning out to be secondary like turning over in their graves.
In my dream paradise is a library.

I am the book reflecting over.
Sequence can happen but never right here.
Poetry secretly knows it is not literature.

Knowing thinking occurring in the blanks tells you the poem is telling all along.

Contact the green fuse force lineal drive.
What is it getting you to the end of halfway there.

Feeling where you put gods a syllable at a time.
It may puzzle but it's not a puzzle.

Never over even as you know it *is*.

Read around.
The poem needs to speak to itselves and requires reading incursion.
Mirror. [*imperative*]

The transferring logic is its grammar out looking.
Marking gods sites. [*verb noun divines*]
Reading deforms an absent text to make room for this one.

Still don't know how to read until read.
Axiality's function displaces intention.
The myth of identity gives itself new credence in *my* work, never mine.

The primary alliance hereabouts is flesh.
Poetic affliction—imaginative literalism.
I never stop wanting to believe my images.

Knowing worship in its green flame I'm gone in.
Everything you succeed in reading here is my failure to believe.
It was a problem then it burned.

Self-made explosives are terrorizing my inner complacence.
My graduality doesn't like being gradual knowing it is anyway.
Along the way grading categories like stone land.

That makes this the site of continuing union never over.
Insane break's humane take.
The cross state renders reader and bone music.

The opening cloud gap closes before you can get your hand through.
Turn of the plow vs. play in the gears.

I'm listening into history as music tracking currents.
My mind so called calls back when called music.

Sounds take pleasure in themselves at our suspense.

Musical bone rhythm runs under rhyme rendered name bound.
A syntax for every thought births.
Rhythm has *truthed*, for ruth, absolute in its instance.

Date grounds what mind grinds.
Language is at play in the fields of the sword.
It's playing with me incisively.

Here where I am most suspended.
It upends.

It can't seem to help playing out its rite celebrating biological identity.
Cheering at a distance. Spooky nature.
Better not have unlived tentacles dangling from our incarnation passing.

Suffering getting here, suffering being here, suffering leaving here, symmetry.
The meaning requires improvisation in accordance.

The most extreme interpretation is more likely than likable.
Zero fringe.

Tone on bone, bone on tone life is turning tables, audibly.
Flesh and psyche still learning how to play together image accordingly.

The feedback system in your hands is polydextrous.
At heart the work is skillless.
Language doesn't exactly exist but it exacts living.

The poem progresses beyond my liking.
My stomach turns on me.
I turn on my text.

Hate words all around my inner all-around guy.
Shorthand for lifelonging longlife.
Light my spire.

Sequentiality shows its fungible head.
Better wed or rather led than said I do *dead.*
Ruthful miserable miracle getting a new spoken lift.

We keep switching vehicles.
The flame world bounds.
Poem consumes itself in its own fire.

Writing to the edge the fear is you're over for keeps.
Frame world burns in drone tone.
Yet the feel's still falling.

There's momentum in the moment and zero plunge.

A music calls a life to its line.
Saying self is feeling itself knowing it's here this time on.

If it's a line it's possible.
It sees itself seeing itself further.

The musician evolves with her instrument reaching over and under.
Real unity is always at variance with itself willing.

Read slow, swallow little.
Thinking non-duality is already dual as all duality is non-dual already at heart.

It's no triumph to be read out of good will.
Bad is another story.

All that moral pressure never gets around to moral.

Music's vocational framing is jobless matrimony.
The subject is in the weave mixing up whose metaphor.

Set free in unlike tunes the sitar outers.
Polydexterity of flesh and psyche, deep confusion made new in few.

Feel full falling.
Absolute is falling further freely.

It takes two to one.

You know it's right because it tells you.
Soon as pen hits page it strips the surface bare.
Insightful saying is a site of citing less

A dharma thing isn't.
No one asked me how long I should be alive here.
Best we can do is get mutual.

One world is disruption.
Emotions won't edit. Not really.
I don't much change unless the magnifying glass edges over. Brighter clouds.

Poetry offers an urge to stop not thinking by ear.
Never to avoid the mix revealing intervallic pace in a moment whole.
Keeping itself apart not to stay small one shows between the parts.

Poetry is dharma without reliable sources.
Reader awareness: how much chaos can you handle.
Not so much meaning as sense swell till it exudes.

Sound bounds out of bounds.
If you need a meaning here it is: it exceeds.
Its too many is not not any, meaningfully speaking.

Identity is at least what cannot be contained in the thought imagining it.
Either you are dharma or it isn't.
When it's double I double.

Why embrace and alienate at once?
Why reject anything when thinking it is for itself?
Everything will be just okay and nothing is or will ever be just so.

A poem births a world where reading births worlds.
It means its happening's happening straight away.
I do I like it because I like it.

The world is the trickster.
My orient got shucked.
Lusions and ludens are.

Reader awareness: how much sight into can you bear?
Saying I am superior naked wears itself heavily.
What's complete already you never complete, get used to it.

Asking you tells me I'm telling you.
A vision is taking hold in seeing.
A miracle is performing itself before your eyes opening.

Worlds slip in and out by the line.
We work the hinge.

Control ills out of control.
It visions language fresh in its verb naturing.

There's weaving fear being out of line in the line midst.
Surrendering is or it isn't or ever.

Our wiser than we are lives limp to alert.
The life line runs through poem being opening eyes ears-first.

Personality is choosing the adopted disorder.
Emotion in the way has sweep, the feel of peregrine falcon stooping.

Hallucinary facts objective dreaming adopt an illness.
Reverie slows down the breathing brain base beat, loosening syntax.

Gap tone. Frown sound. Accent gone. Sun up.
Root centers bringing back into the fall through zone.

Can we detect movements smaller than eyes size?
Take away the question mark and see question for what it is sized.

Language gets straight in a curve.
Rectification magnification signification slanting off.

It's either everything it can be without going that far or not so far.
Dreaming's meaning's happening itself, waking up sleep walking out.

Control ills when out of control's how I'm being here.
This way sound bounds out of bounds.

Word orders itself around getting the right attention.
A line fleshes out just to see.

We've been made.

I want to know what is being said but I can't say what I don't know yet. Patience.
My impersona is in my lap.
It's all happening at once so we're surrounded by language, watch.

The poem writes itself in liquid stone. Okay graphite. Lead.
All at once time mirrors atemporal.
A whole life tune has all the curves curving now with undertow.

Language meditates itself while contemplating nothing.
The book is a present all its own dimension always elsewhere here.

The music walks you out of time.
You change your tune.

This state doesn't know its name.
I know better than to say so is why I do.

Thrown toward telling you how I'm doing it does it make a difference, I'm asking.
Do I have to know my show to be shown how?
No-way knowhow knows better.

A stone throws up the verticality of its moment.
I'd say we make history but it's quicker now.

Sudden updraft.
We gallop to the end.

It's noisy until listening finds its other ear.

11 *lust longs to devote*

I'm busy here creating your hearing me better than I.
This is personal without knowing who.

Take gender as if taking it back to itself.
Identicality's waving in the wind.

She means to me as I am not ever to myself. Yet. But. And.
She sweats me out.

She tears the eye in particles.
Fluid lusting devotion is translucent inherent red waves.

Emotion's motion is always moving in the mind.
It still points to an end.
Stillness completes moving us.

Suddenly I say *the lily is inwardly shielded radiant.*

I and my poem chicken and egg either way or both at once are no matter.
The chicken's dinosaur smart sharpened bird brain I'm evolving.
Thank the egg.

Birth is an intensely aggressive turn for the further.
Egg mirrors other before it sees itselves.

Its tune precedes sound and sad to hear it go.
Grounding before going over. And over.

Clear the mirror my mind wants out.

All afternoon I have been trying to do something other than decide.
I've never experienced being 100% identical to myself for more than a moment.

We organ-obsessed mesopsychs are biologically disposed to not exclude the middle.
We come in thirds.
This is a moment bereft amidst reference failure.

You know in your heart that this statement is not true or false.
No line is self-contradictory before read.
Every line in step with life risks waxing negative before the end.

Time is genuinely confusing in seeming so fake.
How is it possible not to override the verticality of the moment?
Growing aggresses.

Everyone is talking at once so what is there not to understand.
The part of the art that is not art in part is absolutely vertical.
Wherever it is that's anywhere is happening all at once.

The poem is homeless by multiplicity.
Human is looking to the horizon eye leveling.

We're in the mirror and looking out's how the poem knows you're there.
Reading breeds an other reading.

Certainty is dying down making room for the turn over.

Saying *she* is living poetry is necessary for my accurate self-correction.
She calls out the cut.
I get scared. Ecstatic trimming.

Real devotion never looks like itself as when crawling over and out.
Meanwhile one of my obscure beliefs crossed my path as a black cat.

What makes believe in her speaking makes her hidden sitar barely a whisper.

Speaking is the place that allows it to be.

Words get murky contaminated and waking ones attract poems to shake it off.
Intense states languaging that inability to speak partner with still alien ability.
Self-made middle voice isn't calling to recognize ourself otherwise.

Music partners with reader writing edging over.
It hears draping the blank.

We are they who in body are banished from the depths of the sea and reaches of sky.

In your gut you know it's not true or false.

The creamed coffee surfaces a continuum between disgust and sublime.
My three mobile units head, torso, legs going their separate my ways get me here.

Haptic intelligibility has its own linguistic feeling itself in the pen in hand.
No time is this time waiting to be told.

No time owns time's own time.
The tune, not true, not not true, makes the head swirl, and the torso, and the legs.

Hope and fear don't have to come together because they never came apart.
This is the end of the poem without beginning and with middle turning out.
My art is devious, it has me fooled.

The vampire squid from hell screws the ocean swirling self.
The poem has the organs the body gives up, as Artaud attends knowing.
She says try this on—it's more interesting if it doesn't fit.

Our strangeness is hidden by our gendering rage for word order.
Contrariness is danceable.

Here we are nuanced from trouble to trouble.
Life is the gift of an interim touch literacy by ear beside itself in tone bliss.
A slide by meaning too fast to crit.

Revelation through feedback from scratching it out.
Poetry is a crisis of faith.

It cites rites with critical edge.
Faithful slice and continual splice.

We reflect obverse self passage from here.
Energetic palpation of a threat treats.

Never knew being in a place knows no again.
That's why we can't stop coming back here where we've never been.

I posit *her* because it is the nature of this place to do so, be so.

15 *years learning the art of indifference*

I write on this spot, earth, page, belonging to a place yet to be seen.
Please intoxicate me over my limit.

I confess to spilling my blood.
Being verse never turns sanitary.

My two sides in one rest are at long last learning to play together.
If you've come this far you know the point is not knowing where you are.
Both ways at once is the secret direction.

It's not playing fair if you damage the goods getting nowhere.
The thing of beauty is a joy with a lever.
The musician smiles in the smiling parts.

Say everything at once like all the people speaking, it's party time in no time.
I've been a holdout, death is saying.

I'm still reading the strong book having shifted to the weak.
Repressing beauty rouses turning.

The reach of a poem is the wash of a breath.
In your heart you know genius is—alien to all.

I'm not my thoughts, except maybe some bad ones, fuel, lead, chrysalis.
The body is not as poem is not a totalitarian society—it listens to unreason.

In order to un-*what word will*-reason well.
If you hear it it's there.

I'm not still a fish.
I have loving deadlines precariously retaining the end before I even begin.
How can my aberrant inner many ever get along with evolving poles afield?

It's not ethical to believe in advance. Nor make believe.
Seduced by the image I study from afar, horizon copulates with seer.
Living world makes a living world wise.

Goat foot rhythm on a hill my size.
The surface you hear in the mirror mirrors.
Lines are cross-questions showing wedunit.

Visual cues ensemble listening scores timing advancing.
Verbal objects watch out for themselves.
We're catching ourselves at a moment remembering ourselves for the first time.

The frame is what you look out through being looked at too within.
Tune around and down through.
I live in a shoe with one foot forward.

The unspeakable stretches.
This is the sense in that the music is singing talking back.
Words figure out how to live showing on the page.

Marks on the march carry the message to our future ant hill convergent evolution.
We're talking our way into diagonal nature.

Time is not but I fail to see it that way.

There are mysteries that don't bother being mysterious, the beat goes off.
How do you let the thing you're loving get here being a thing?
A lyric to a song with a very long lip shaping, and moody.

Inside reading hangs around cracks.
Trips between lines line in.
The thing on the page things further.

When it speaks to you you're spoken through.
Up and down the sitar strings string.
Effect affects facts sing-song.

What's it trying what you're thinking.
Persistence in writing persists in recalling calling.
Sooner or later we come to the part where the contradictions have sex. Release.

Identity surrenders to microtone sounding unheard of. Relax.
Movietone is remembering childtime.
May body and mind get in step for a change.

The music changes more than the outfit.
Mating at hand happens with wand.
Person voice speaks writing for itself.

It's frigid outside when it's frigid inside.
Friction in diction beats the heat out by lip.
Alienation heals the thought *healing*.

You never want to go in from play.
I'm reassured by present uncertainty, at least in longing.
It's like reading fate in the quality of exhaust, vehicular.

Captives can't quit.
Some are best known in their non-ordinary, ragged raga lettering.
Alienation gives birth new, cutting close.

No more drift along religio flow back.
Why hang on meaning when it wants to hang on you.
Can it take you by its throat?

It's learning its language at my expense and now at yours.
Wake the fuck up she says.

It's a stray with mirror.
Eve ate first and Adam fell happy.
This is as looking back as I get.

What am I thinking I was thinking, never ask and never ask to think.
Evolving is turning out the coming outcome, all out.
Slow down to see how it speeds up.

Now marks time midpoint between (never) catching up and (never) getting ahead.
The species imagines itself forward just where it is.
Where you come in is where you get back out, if ever.

You come back to where the raga never ends.

19 *dualism's gas in the tank*

Disgust recapitulates phylogeny.
Vilém Flusser, *Vampyroteuthis Infernalis*

Lift off! I become what I project.
Felix culpa or happy to be falling if that's what this is.
Alienation is a joy forever.

Will we ever join forces with transindividuating life forms hill-dwelling and hives?
Poetry is species puppetry. In denial.
E.g.: We true animals rarely experience how outnumbered we are by protozoa.

We distance ourselves by measures of disgust like a gust of wind.
Everything feels itself first.
If reality is radial every word touches every other word no matter what page where.

Walking heads on the bottom of the ocean and many legs, many selves, verbals.
Thinking of them inspects us.
The alien philosopher is laughing his way into poetry, verbal gusts.

His love is like a headfoot rising.
Proprioceptive blind faith suggests patchlife quilt, quite stable.

Gusting along Buddhism is a stray against the present background.

Don't bother waking the fuck up she said, too late.
Reflexive Dasein rebottles with your inner genie.

TOO LATE!

If you don't want your mind fucked with don't read this.

Poetry is a double cross load.

Patchwork guilt makes patchlife quilt.
Flicker-effect of syllabic sleight.
Saussure sure sees language funny sans scribble, says she selling seashells.

Funny feeling on raw tongue has its own unknown song.
We do the things putting gas in the tank.
If only we would take the time to read what it's saying, so sure. No doing.

No fooling but dead serious.
I'm changing my attitude, Mr. James, and this is what it takes.
The poem takes in what is giving out.

The mystery of dying on the table lies.
The ways of reading are the ways of being back where you start.
The ragged raga reading seeding sways on.

Every word counts in its syllable doubles falling off in ones.
This is no vacation but it vacates.
Gust dust disgust mind degrades.

Life is in denial of death and no doubt vice versa.
Would it were other as it is.
No one's going no where.

You understand it's mind minding its business gaps.
You can sing along following the bouncing belly.
It tells like a telly.
Silly sails are secretly willies.

I'm trying to make this count, but it hasn't taken to number or drugs neither.
This is a one shot.

The configuring is personal like mescal and the ways of having a body.
The numbers are laughing at us behind our backs.

Time is tired in us.
It lays us about in anxiety *flagrante*.

Flamenco knows its raga like sex death in eternity.
You never know when it'll hit you that the bolt's never stopping.

We're free to choose not to know but can we forget we do?
It doesn't promise I'll like it here.

Mind gets tricky like a trick knee.
Heat got me in the jumping place.

This is one shot & one shot.
Illness teaches.

Pulse times a speaking music.
No one is higher than any other one let alone two.
Three ones is one three.

That is one shot & one shot & one shot.
Never right or wrong but thinkable maybe.
Still itching for a flight yet stitching through the night.

Staring into the cream swirl in the coffee I see my passion to be looked back at.
Things verb in their eyes vibe.

I did best I could but less than thought, flew any way.
Think safe.

High and dry I'm withdrawing from my devotional bank.
Spent absence is verbal payout in the nick of time.

Symptomatic syntactics alerts your healing feelings.
This is the news from our brief visit on your planet.

Birth is a Faustian bargain from the beginning before *you* even get there.
Soft shoe with aura shows.

Listening in on the music solicits infinity.
Binding lines the bounding line restoring balance for all of a moment.

At the tip of your wave you mean it all.
At the fold you recuperate body.

No point arguing what's not pointing.
The longing between lines voices urgent incarnation.

No more drifting soap opera to soap opera, take this short cut no soap radial.
The impersona is who you say you are coming from behind.

I'm looking at myself looking at you but neither of us fits the mirror.
Verb vibe is a matter of seeing what you hear.

You'd think it didn't matter seeing the musicians playing but listening to their eyes.
Vibrant mattering's reserved for those who come for what was never heard.

I call it moly folly when I don't know what I'm saying.
I can't get ahead of its voice without falling back to the beginning.

Every line has a myth going.
It departs in what arrives.

The words you could say suffer murmuration.
There's no outside but what bounds your thinking on the spot.

Thoughts do not follow in the order of their coming.
Check the undertone that fits the word like bone and hollowing.

It has the sacred authority of puddles mirroring your face back to sky.
This is drifty thinking but the tug's coming from center behind, no way you see that.

Don't look back Orphée now that we know it's impossible not to.
Seeing yourself in Mercury has consequences.

Losing track of the thought mirrors the other track, no point stopping.
There's always the flip side passing over.

Fact is it's happening in voice giving you leave by attraction.

I entered a climate of belief like a low-pressure system.
It's got its own theme song hearing you coming.

Why can't I see pictures that aren't taking me?
It takes patience riding a wave you can't see.
Saying around turns you around.

I moved house to a better belief.
Climate ranges.

Three steps in you become the neutralizing mirror.
The music is playing you.

Mirror being fires back what is firing on.
The book writes the poem as the map maps its own territory.

It does what it does with you in mind.
We tried talking to god like this but I'm still not her listening.

I'm waiting for the permission that's never not given not ending.
It's the set up in the sustainable self.
Entering the adjacent climate tells how textural we are.

There's a music not listened to that listens through you.
It wants more through the more you want.

It's only here bothering you to be said.
Learning its language starts by its learning you.

I keep hoping to find my hero in her in here.
It's never let me think this before.
A line is not like her body but her body is lining here.

The curve is the way I'm seeing it hearing.
The aura aromas.
Playing in the music to hear it all at all. Stumble.

My hollow hollers like two steps neutral.
Picture it picturing itself.
Words sweat.

Read inside what plays out inside.
The end of days colors red on this side.

Effect strived for never stops striving.
Music introspects by way of mirrors.

If you think hearing it it hears.
Not bound hand and foot by my horizon.

It's not always like.
We're talking the space between.

Suddenly feeling an earth inside the horizon keeps me away moving on.
I take no responsibility for what can't even name itself yourself.
Take three. It's how to have having done.

I keep coming back to the place where I first met me.
The simplest mind stake stalks me here.
Return is to vaginal awareness as sense of being born missed the first time round.

The poem is a knowing cure.
It's letting me know what I can't yet think.
Poetic is knowing even less for sure.

Rilke's tower's where no characterization touches home.
Windows with arms going out celebrate what they can't be seen as.
The connection with the past is only sudden.

Listening tells the tone to tell like a morning bell.
You don't see it if it's not personal.
Escapist horizon. Not me it. Missing the working verb.

Nostalgia for language drives language from the past by irruption.
No drift along religio.
You know it's right and you don't know why.

First it strikes you now.
Out of nowhere is alive and well.
It means the way the tongue curves and she catches the wave.

Sweet words sweat most.
Their best sentence evades thinking best.

It's how it shows a sense of accuracy not from sense of sin.

What I'm saying is said before I say it not before now.
My one point is coming at me.
Still not mine and never is the only thing still to claim.

No point trying to remove the blemish, coming and going is its own.
Beneath the surface we grasp for metaphors to breathe.
We swing our arms to confirm the space.

Seemingly getting together with myself for a real talking to through.
This sense of presence posits nothing, substantially.
The players acknowledge the music to make music.

Unless you never want it to stop you never get it.
Crawling up inside her strings you get plucked.
If it finds you it finds where you've found you.

Putting the emphasis where it makes sense is as startling as nonsense rightens.
This is how I think I am not what I think I think.
The syntax comes with removes moving within, catching on on the go.

It's an area of confidence to freely fall away from yourself in.
No true fit fails to be awkward from the start.
She signals with her body getting out from under all history, musically.

The rhythm is never just from itself, justice in her other never alone.
Simplify deity until thoughtless ruggedly out.
I know it only as I've never heard it.

You can't hear it but the music is running in background.
Marriage I know is teaching, grounding with outback.

When allowed to vary the speaking speaks up direct.
Out of place is the only way into place.

The running is in the background of the underground and a little to the left today.
The joy is it's there even when it isn't here.

Horizon by the line is anywhere along moving away.
It listens for you moving away.

Why fight knowing the gods you make?
Art keeps me young making me old.

You don't carve out a status of reality the way you do wanting.
You're not who you are until the music plays you.

Don't ask *when* when axiality obviates time sense.
Clock time misses the point. Dot. *Point final.*

The young make me told and it's telling,

Time to hear again is how time is.
Jostle me back here where I'm listening through, you could say to you.

Suddenly I have no questions and only questions with fervor.
Quiet, fear, you're being mediated dreaming off again.

How are you talking yourself into a *real* swelling.
I go back and put a comma after real, still swelling.
Now a very slim gap opens between graphemes receding before your eyes.

We happen this way in part because we say we do. It tells you to.
Take the on out of light being thrown (gap) and see where you land.
This is a sentence situation banking on backing up in time.

It follows one's own language never before happening as it is right here, no more.
A new music hears in a new linguality to know its place.

I'm hearing at an angle even when it's bottomless.
Why is it necessary to say again there's no again.
Nevertheless I keep expecting to see the same ol' jackal show up on the back porch.

The strange makes me pull by the logic revealing.
Settle in the swirl's real.
The state may be for sale but the state of being sails toward the horizon.

The score tracks the song on the way here.
Perceptions of the end come in the beginning toning.

Timing ears, time's only again's off the trail of never before.
The waver in the voice serves at the pleasure of mind.
Déjà vu what's not.

It's hard to trap what understands its nets.
We're in the map feeling guided by what it folds out.

Never mind which one.
Still not hearing enough more.

Pretend I know what it's saying in order to feel better, then don't.

A stumble is not a fumble but a quick uptick down under.
Self direction torques perceptual perfection.

Being myself I can't help corrupting myself.
Keep breathing as if you ever never stopped.

Sudden swirl of mind bespeaks the kind still filling.
Remaining empty, what's left at center, here where we enter, more other.

How many functions can word on the head of a pen.
History is the part of the present that won't let you alone.

This makes me a lost cause for Western culture thanks to its lost cause.
The beginning is unstoppable.

The poem advances with its reader by an as yet undefined organism.
Likewise a self-respecting question leaves off its mark.
This is about agreement.
Absence can't help agreeing even to think it.

Reading agrees to the extent anything is read.
The which this is to say infinitely more.

What's your problem with beauty, yogi, but fear of not being right for it.
Mapping what's not yet here and never left.

It's the poem in its drive to speak unthinking.

I am my reader even before my reader is.
My reader knows me less that I know her saying her.

Who knows what angel works in the arts of skin?
How much more intimate without the thought of evil.

I know it's real when it pushes me away.
I'm the horizon where I sit.

Mirrors alter.
Runaway process does not involve running away.

The poem imitates horizontal gene transfer in a vertical kind of spinning way.
It's letting know it knows what's going on even when you don't.

But this doesn't mean me.
It doesn't even mean itself.

What is thought in order relives its disorder.
Word order is never not ordering thought in whatever order.

Reading it is covariation.
How we got here is still getting here.

32 *the strange goddess sees through you*

Not to write experimentally but to live so
and let it speak for itself.
Ontononymous the Particular

When her eyes roll heads roll.
Both ways at once are and not.

The poem tricks me into saying what she intends with me.
I'm escaping what escapes inside coming out.

Water in the voice, earth in the mirth.
Complexity is inevitable, may as well dance to where we're heading no aiming.

I keep mirroring other.
It's changing changing.

No repeats. No.
Suction without seduction lets settling through.

When she speaks we do the mapping, no napping, no saying no.
What is this need to exploit every exciting idea impulse?

The drive to *more* circles the lake back to start.
We're over the top before we start.

Never are we through going through thoroughly, literally.
Choosing your meaning means contrary dogmas agreeably.

Weighted finding has a swing.
It doesn't say it until you let it.

Watch how this happens from the reverse side, she instructs, by pulse.
Right-handedness is now boring, penetratingly through.
I'm taking my verisimilar language as good as it gets out in public.
The very thought of speaking true over all and out there haunts wholeheartedly.

We've been everywhere going nowhere.
You can't deny it without its denying you.
This is the standard for clarity in nonordinary ordination.

Glossodiversity comes with a costly drive in *more* worth its weight in sound.
Feel the middle swing, think double in words and curve of sword.
We're talking biology and this is its movie.

Intelligence is strange to itself and never told where to be.
What is personal in poetry invents language inside language with skin in the game.
Holding is in common.

I can't understand the words but the colors understand in me.
There's a middle waking not committed to its limit meaning.
One moment possessed, one moment possessual.

Axis focuses sidedness in between.
Never spineless and no battle rattle.
She only says what she can't.

Constraints are everywhere, hands free and hands held.
Heart felt palms down and mind at large.
I am my body too, she says, speaking, no doubt for me as if by me.

Coming or going? and do you even know?
How do you say this in your language if you do?

Wing pulse rhythms by which we hear flight tones.
Whole verbs.
Screens are for disappearing in plain sight.

You come in a focusing pulse taking it from there.
Birds were words once heard.
Screened acts of touch touch me.

We're looking at a side.
You can see a mind with music.

If I withdraw from the middle I draw the middle back out.
I'm here hearing what I can't.

All I ever do is answering asking.

Voluntary psychosis is perspective by incommensurability.
The music comes out of the body by way of the tongue sprung.

Aiming to be clear in clearing a way through here in the clear.
Not getting anywhere still comes home in tone.

Mirrors don't talk back taking you in to im*press* you into accepting.
Time of seeing lays not up treasures showing through it.

Facing in reads you facing out.

mirroring by alterity

for Jerome Rothenberg

A poem writes itself in no time round.
Where it goes tabla hangs in the ripple, lining.
Catching mind before it hits bottom there where tone rises as we speak.

This is my best uneducated guess and it knows you didn't ask for what you get here.
You still can. And can't.

There are no contradictions in the same moment but here.
No same moment or not.

My mirror is uncomfortable with me so I'm in retention mode.
The transmission is indirect on paper but the sound imagines being heard.

You never catch the angle where she sees through you mirroring.
Why *she* you ask like me.

So to speak has a certain status in my school of wish.
Writing is truer when your guard is down so to speak.

Reading is truer when the writing is still going on unguarded.
Not happening proves happening.

It has no evolutionary adaptive value and it spreads wings.
Mirror blushing is neuronic sex and hypnautical.

Rare beauty is rare to itself.
It catches bottom up and no small change.

Too wild to mean and too true not, telling laws wear us.
Heartbreaking irony tells on us from behind.
I've been suspending understanding because I never had it, not really.

Deciding what is meant is a moment of utter freedom.
Here goes front to back as the poem mirrors.
Time to mic the drone. Follow the bouncing musics.

Resisting time is my sign of uselessness.
Seeing too much the world is stilling.
Identity dangles my best modifiers.

Titularity crosses me instructing by cheerful affront. I turn back.
What is not yet a word knows it should be. At any cost.
I'm making up my happy mood the way she stood in the door.

She's the goddess of invention according to inmost desire. I know what's mine now.
The discipline is unobjectionable bending *ir*regardless irrespective.
Soft grammar like unto soft body. Did I half hear ire?

Energy flows where you're least liking, no likes blocking.
There's no justification for enjoyment, proved.
Why spend so much time justly not knowing. Question marks.

There is discourse just being swept away.
Reading is sweeping and adjusting on the wry.
It has its breed lineage willing.
It evolves to select her selecting.

I've been hit by minds.
The people are coming and going in *Jerusalem.*
The difference is some know. They have *and.*

It's not what but how we know it.
A work has your life by the throat.
I take it in hand with a sense of land.

Feel the weight, as this late date weighs.
This is how it matters, knowing matter.
Intelligible array with intel astray.

I don't believe the poem is a god except when the poem does, instantaneously.
I suffer it to suffer for me.
It transacts by subtraction.

The verb to be is still discovering how to be [mind to come].
How know itself from the song of effort or the aggression of birth.
Poem's language going blind letting me see.

How to speak ahead without the point of function in hand.
It skirts sounding.
It's scarcely a lane going down.

Who knows how it gets us going down its alley.
Integrity shows at the point of integration in a flash.

The feel of the line is the lineament fining in the current.

4 *for the birds*

The feel of her lines
Evolution defines
Ontononymous the Particular

How many cancelled impulses for fear of beauty the trivial?
And how do you make this thing talk?

Word vehicles for mind eversion wildly torque like duck penises.
Sooner or later the world seeps through the armor.

Just when you think it's over an estranged current hits from the blind side.
Cancel ecstasy merely to evolve no way.

There are no attitudes left to fall for falling free.
Unfold the feeling you can't escape, lean into the curve.

How many dulled impulses for fear of pleasing trivially.
Thinking unscrews.

What if the concept entropy is going into disarray right under your nose.
The agreements are in and out of place.

The mothership lands voicing.
Line issues, birth aggresses, nothing resolves.

Any instant being proves no proof.
Oppositions illude.

Speaking from inside bats wings.
It takes us apart and gives start.

the thought protects

People may be unfitted by being fit in unfit fitness.
Kenneth Burke

Why interpret my dream when the dream is interpreting me?
We have an appointment so you can't possibly be late.

My avenue bowers to keep me showing indominant, right words won't do.
Unminding evolution betters far worse.

Accepting the absence of language is a start with startle.
Humans are animals that manufacture opposition in excess of biology.

Birds steal, ducks rape, escape is the wrong idea.
Beauty over survival desires over fear.

I feel a non-functioning formal fit coming on.
It's for the birds, must be ours too.

Starting to erode the contrary powers hiding us.
Backwash is not backlash.

Birth starts *off.*
Hearing pulses wing gestures, breaking optional.

Female preference is not limited to gender distinction not being one-sided.
Perspective by incongruity tones incommensurably specific.

Male club-winged manakins of Ecuador sing with wings like nobody's business.
Interspecificity is troubling happily doubling.
Think mirror altering specifics.

I am not recovering from the threat of poetry.

Real agreements are never prior.
I'm raising questions through my narrow chink from their dead.
Phonemic slant means by odds.

Think a universe neither absurd nor not but neutrally opportunistic.
Minding evolution worsens better.
Just making our way happily astray.

There are thoughts that leave a hole where they came out.
Any doctrine of resonance hides its doctrinal solids in the current.
Is this or that bedrock truth anyway?

There's language that never stops crawling around your head.
Exposure of biological architecture implicates the maker in display.
These blocks move around, happy haptics.

The hard problem explaining's longing.
Learning the alphabet is endless no less.

Our no order thinking appears to be getting the upper hand, as lower hand spills.
The peacock disappearing in the bush leaves his colors behind.
Resonance by negation goes so far, then the embrace takes shape at the horizon.

You disappear.
Time is a healer killer.
Consciousness is self-evident and now what.

Poetry is nature teaching itself to speak in the singular collective.
I've got it in hand holding to layering thought by burst of fickle feeling, so ours.

A page turns by the word.
It feels a wayfare electric.

How can animals not have anima if you do, if you do?
Caveat lector.
Alphabetical authority may be missing in action but don't stop looking.

Words turn in page proving.

Language's catachresis (I'm stretching, feel strained) is a matter of perspective.
Style is how it fails to get away from us.
Brain laundering is the other side of money.

Thoughts deflect while mirroring what page collects.
Childhood is the mnemonic for irresistible incompletion.
The strangeness of dying is accurate response to unthinkable non-being.

God gave me such a fright I took him for the devil in disguise. And so.
Childhood remembers itself in me.
O to be 20 again but without the agenda.

The page declares what I can only think floating down my river.
I mourn the moment.

Unoriginal sin is the only kind.

8 *red is for knowing ahead still unprepared*

The order is how the mark goes down on the way out.
The state of mind colorates stating mind.
The effort is not getting in the way.

Communication relies on an unspoken undercurrent in undertime, wary of rapids.
I cry out when I can't bear my thought.

By habit we forget the outside is not all out.
The painter lives a double life with one foot on planet Paint.

The wish knows more rooms in the infinite possible multiverse imaginized bright.
The work tells you what to think before taking it away.

This is knowing life is a disguise for what only it knows.
You have to live it beyond acceptable to find out what.

More, more! means I'm not all here till the paint dries.
The future is dawning already in the mind of the lines.

Awe is more than suspicion it's coming as we follow.
What does the work ask but that you ask it to work you?

Art slows things to their eternity.
The artist's discipline is never reaching an eternal thing alone.

Take me to your reader, we're new here.
A jeweled rider on a horse descends the arch of a lama's hat *just* for now.

You might be the one! Language of the gods.
Art would talk back to them through them through us.

We are no one.
The elect are they who forget to get elected.

I give you my one double life lived with one foot on the planet Word.
Ordinary objects keep losing their names strangely saving us the strange.

We're reading about life as we live it, but we keep our feet on the sound.
Every sentence owns a possible raga in what it can't possess.

Forgetting how to spell the simplest wurd alerts you to the threat of language.
Thought slippage is a twisting tongue wriggling to be free.

You're not stupid, says the poem, just not looking back up and out at once.
No flagging says the inner non-language orator.

It's Sunday until the sun sets in the word.
I declare myself student pre the verb to which saying so surrenders.

It's someday all the livelong day.
Hilaritas means the joke is on me.

Time to hear genius out of its bottle despite the insufferable rattle.
A god who sees *through* you *sees* through you.

Selves are at large again.
Call the hounds we need their sounds.
It's our nature's need to redound.

I will still be a probable me till I get to the end *here*, where I think to be.
Mind interfaces with all, blood & guts & the brainy other other.

I give you my leader where the sun won't blind.
Do we really need to know where it's coming from and would that even help?

Predation precedes seduction.
Jury's out on evolution as a journey beyond coercion, ask the birds.

The inner need for scripture is in full rupture *flagrante*.
You know there's an inner child feeling remembered as the scroll unrolls.

It tells our story and we can't resist, who ever asked to virginate?
Scribe takes time to the absurd, and don't believe a word, you've been served.

Thought protests resisting.
Evolution by plumage hypnotic erotic dances to her tune.

Picking up on wing pulse gestures by ear.
Nature includes the measured belief that teaching *is*.

Defiant science is a blood art.
Perspective by incommensurability inhering here where thou art, hot scripted.
Raga rages in the very pages turning to sign.

Life on a dime is a page turner.
Will you still be you by the end of the line?

Genius is the active side of listening.
Showing new in a close shave near you.

Prayer is that my confusion benefits and I get to say Lord knows how.
Good Buddhists love approval in spite of.

Evidence is God created Eve from Adam's boner *baculum* to cut him down to size.
4.5 inches is the average dubious news yet so much worry.

Evolutionarily, he came at her with his structural beam support and she leveled him.
If she had to wait for safe truth she'd never say anything.

Soon a poetics will be reduced to a rubric of its accomplishment.
Bang for the buck is relative to buck banged.

Excuse me while I give birth to a new past moment.
I'm building a bower for her still unborn self, probable as can be.

Art works unseen analogous to cryptic female choice, o savior.
I'm scarcely the me I remember.

My fastfooted future still rips from nerve ends.
I thought I knew who I thought I was but now I don't think so.

Haphazardously pregnant with a stillborn past ends the instant you know it.

Listening for blue I see louder.
Imagine a line of thought as cell of a thoughtful field, its end is its beginning.
To say this kind of thing is to mean it in a cellular memory sense changing.

If the thinking line is long the mind is barely itself halfway on.
The past's still riding the synapse bare.

There's no accounting for being right here.
A cell is no particular size but breathes with its place.

Literal things are not themselves literalist.
I'm redirecting my past for future eyes ready for striptease, if you please.

You don't literally become what you read as no mirror reverses up & down.
Ground swells by looking, we switch, converse further on each other's side.

Your mind stays with its mind staying with possible reading pulse edging in flare.
Ratio evolves.
The past in line is not safe from invention in the read back.

Past sense is past syntactic grasp, throwing up of hands.
I sense rational mind jumping past conclusion.
Who knew we were just waiting for the next dance step tonal flip.

No one can help living small.
Single sense is too great expense.

I have no time for this and *no time* has me letting go.

Today a poem taught my nerves new tricks.
The simplest words can tongue tie tangling with their inherent variability.

I'd lay back but the heat has my feet on the move like Hatlo's Inferno underfoot.
Evolutionary science at long last can think female sexuality inherently variable.

Discovering nuances of relationships existing as of now reorients the middle ear.
A thing in its place is an absolute.

You don't get to be you relatively.
Eye to eye we become each other's transmogrifying mirror.

Turnkey happiness hazes by way of consensus.
On the other lip double meaning doubles in the root.

How many issues can dance on the ear of a syllable, I'm listening.
No question you live inside questions.

Two days pass and the sentence poises to continuing uproot, timelessly forward.
We don't hear ourselves speak with the same ears twice.

The joy is that it happens and you hand with two hearts the sudden frame.
Verging on assertion the capture floats you back on your back.

Other mirrors on your other edge.

Waking awareness heads for trouble yet filters the news.
Excitable in neutral spins the vehicle's up & down at once.

I'm learning to play for the free to play.
Measured by measuring in the patter pointing spaces on.

A poem neither does nor does not stand up to its statements.
It can think so as not to be thought yet bounding.
It shaves not losing edge in course.

Hearing a thought as thought among thoughts fails to enter its turbulence.
I let go, it lets me go, it goes.
Ice flows.

The poem takes away even that which it gives for keeps.
Evolutionary function supports removing supports.
Reading is expecting agreeing not to.

Blanking in.
Tune tone tentation is trying.
Thinking filters.

Once surfacing's at once for all and always.
Any particle speaks up for the grammar passing through.
Waking awareness drives into the storm with evasive maneuvers.

Impermanence is the mode of operation responsible for multiverse at play.
It passes fast while not passing at all.

I take refuge in the instant present about which this lies.

The poem asked me to spell out to her the poetics of excitable neutrality.
Request mirrors what my many apparent selves require.
Syntax describes how it cuts short.

Intensity comes on a grade on a wave.
The music is a full-scale event on site in curve.

Rhythm is the rate of receipt.
Excitable in neutral never stops once spinning.

Variable vows upend unending.
Read the sentence from the middle layflat core streamed forth & back turning.

Speed is not intrinsic but absolute happening.
Layers lining in & out & still in flow.

Life describes itself keeping in track.
Lines layer laid out flat.

You're seeing from above at eye level, the god's why view.
Seemingly gods shy too as we see what we do.

Reading isn't stopping while it does.
Principled zone of non-limiting holds instant presently.

Bounding bounds.

Born to tell your tale is swimming without your tail.

Unfamiliar seems wrong minus the song.
History is convinced repetition.
Another day all shot to hell minus the telling.

Sentence is not thought but thinking in forming.
See if you can say life outflanks by way of blank.
Ice light doesn't show the flow.

Why convince history to repeat when we can shag it in the act.
Timely can produce other against the grain.
The secret message is it's possible.

The poem you see is but an example of itself.
No original matches.
It says what isn't understood.

You don't see the wind in the trees not wishing to be seen.
Tabla eyes sitar irrupting.
If you need a reason for doing it it's given.

The dogma is a lens and a lens cap.
Saying in the dark is seeing in the mouth and wary tongue.
Pretending suspension is the one throne, toning.

Sweet science is the sentence knowing the world for you in you too.
She's here to sort you, in between you & you.

Being goes all the way down.

It gives you what you can give focused in another tense, untensing.
Equanimity in disequilibrium disqualifies the inequitable equation. Swallow.
How he shakes hands differs from how he shakes his hand, pure.

Confucius goes without saying.

Discrimination by music hears even defectual being harmoniality.
We're driving down the road kicking up a storm on our wayward after here.
Syntax is what tells me, tripping *up*. Get that straight.

It makes me back up saying.

On the other hand direction confuses us.
Get permission from the tongue lest it refuse to say *thus*.
Enjoying health is quiet bliss self wishing well.

We don't count, at least not numerically.
Pulse particulates embodily.
No bottom to being.

Pace partitions between apparent and functional contradictions, if you follow.
A function focus is a function of focus.
It gets hot enough to heal.

Being fails to bottom out.
The poem bodies out for it.

I caught myself convincing history to repeat, tongue out flat.
How can such simple elements lie in so many directions at once?

A note states, gonglike.
Discourse is a highrise rarely rising high, with flats.

To see a thing is to only have been looking.
Flat lot shout, in a manner of singing, *your lot laid out.*

Poem is rescue action outspoken.
Song fake originates.

If the field does the singing *the ring signs to wield.*
Power punctuates from afar.
Nonsense powers the possible.

I speak in principle in season.
Reason seasons as song singles.

Intention is another level of invention rising.
Daimon is its principle wished under time.

Sucked out of wet wood, just saying having my way with weald.
Grace catching on the leave.

Faking living is grammar on the make.
B♭ Mass wherein a thing has its music to make, forsaken.
Cross time out back making over.

cultivating inconsistencies

The harder you fall,
the higher you bounce.
Chandler Chapman

Please pass the bottle my mind is hovering.
A genie is pretending to be me again, I'm on guard.

How far can you get interior to the music, speakably.
How far can a mind hold to the center without lowering the shades.
Wondering is questioning yourself inseparable from interiors to come.

Agreement need not include agreeing.
A logic is a mode of mind mood aiming to sustain itself legit.
Not reading has momentum.

The subject verb relation keeps stressing itself.
Say one thing mean four plus subtractions.
The number is just a member.

A line is what's possible to live through the instant stretching.
It's learning to count over and over no end no lie.
Music instructs the instrument instructing the instrumentalist.

At the top anyone is an amateur for whom birth is appearance.
Music says any*things* able to be said together.
Not to mention retractions except spontaneously conceived. Weave.

Anything said so as to be heard instructs in its music never having been said.
Being flat mass has bounce once now.

Interruption hearing itself has momentum in renounce.

Even if you knew what it all means you'd ask what it all means.
Inquiring self-generates.

I have successfully romanticized my actions, so they tell me.
Actions speak more verbally than words.
Believing the music is the music of dark places.

Resisting repeating is getting out of the way of deafening momentum.
Music by contraries suckles my vagaries.
Gut feeling sounds its slush with swirl aiming.

Thinking is humming to itself tuning up throughout the tune.
The song captures its lack.
She'll shell so you dwell singing at the corner of thinking dimensions.

Believing hypnosis shows the hypnosis of belief.
Poem models how we talk to ourselves by way of other hearings.
Key attributes don't stick out.

Belief edits and radiates like science hypnosis.
Radial meaning you can't keep hold of briefly revels.
Conscious belief evolves consciously while still believing unconsciously.

No need to search out the connections ever in search of themselves.
If it happens it happens, if not not, so to speak.
Seeing before is not now seeing nor not.

Alive now sees everything ever created is for me not just me.

I showed up like a bat out of hell in the mirror.

No help for trying to paint the outside knowing what it is.
Who knows who knows.
Poetry drives the unconscious to surrender.

Quicksilver quickens connection reflection.
For a moment I knew I'd met me before.
I trip over my fixations.

Reductivity is withdrawal out of fear.
In a flash a color disappears.
A thing has mantra when speaking in its own sound.

Channels reroute to feel the flow through true.
Meeting life halfway is not geometric so much as geothermal.
Every line a flash with own duration, sit out the unflashing.

Energizing disorders.
Feel the pulse as if stone lives.
When reading slows the edges flow.

Life self watching is the movie seeing its maker.
Underline water's pouring into the waterway thinking.
Simple is flash without limit.

Putting mind on the line is risky necessity.
When it goes hands free and all verbals flying there's no chance.

I can't always meet my poem halfway.

Poetry is language seen living this once.
Think flesh that flesh think speaking.

I don't mean this but I am meant to say it saying this.
Identity dilates.

No chance this works for a living.
A line leaves no calling card.

Time stands still until you spook it.
Recentering is by the line.

Poem surrounds mind over time.
Energy orients over and over, timely.

I can't always meet my life halfway.
The present dilates.

When the poem goes fans free and all verbals chancing it it's flying.
My conception feels the tide going out.

The raga finds its way continuing.
What's personal is the way you know it knowing you.
No alone but all alone and one.
Reentering is by mirror both ways.

I talk to myself in a foreign language not all of us listeners know.
Poetic flight from the world makes trouble on its own wings.

Cross rhythms mirror neuronic cruxification.
Complexity bleeds fuel with swirl.

Poem resembles life as what occurs at the intersection, crash included.
Colors intensify disappearing themselves.

Line trails including ahead.
The music's ahead coming this way residually.

A dip in discourse in time to invent a new way to think.
The poem feels happy when we stop trying to order the world at its threshold.

Reality generating language—think mirroring.
I turn it upside down so it shows up.

Suddenly my face is my detractor and it's not me but my live-in critic.
Shifting syntactic agency is just how it is the way we are flexing.

Bottom up we're half-way to saying nothing at all—bottom out.
The human race with its races races to the end.

Body expresses what it meets and tangling to no end.
It answers to itself inside the world out.

It makes the sense that stops making sense.

This is the other way it could be said.
I distance myself the closer I get here.

Mind can't stop playing with itself.
No two birds hold the same birder the same.

I know birth while I can't find my birth.
My body is dragging me through my sentence.

Self made mind trickery.
Poem can't stop playing with itself including the reader.

This is the other way it could have meant to be meant to be.
The rose that is a rose is the rose still eating Adam's apple.

Sense is not made but born.
Instantly breathing is the source of confusion.

Does saying *kill two birds* send shivers through the trees?
The rare eagle flapping wings in the mind is rarer release from fear.

No dead measure rhythm striates brain wave.
Incremental pulsation distributes parcours particulates.

Every linearity a possible poem waiting to happen like breath.
Heart channels bleeding out front.

Feeling is at a loss for worlds.

My art would be that of living:
each moment, each breath is a work inscribed nowhere.
Marcel Duchamp

My deep past is as gone as the beginning of this sentence and not.
How can we stand these ceaseless reversals but as twisters in tongue the more.

I'm at a loss for word worlds.
Poem houses.
If it's near I feel it feeling in me.

Pleasure pounces in the big cat metaphor.
Psychosis without tears.
Tricky mind self made over over and over.

Verbal shivers I mean to say happen.
The poem expects good will willing otherwise modally.

A world wants you to want its approval.
A world is found wanting or not at all.

Playing with numbers shows the toy side of cumulative things.
One world one swirl.
The clock doubles for real time, duplicitously.

Reading I'm on this side of my page longing toward another.
It proposes a doing that sees itself without question.

Firstness brings confusion to the edge.
As the myth arises into its own distinction stomach breathes a little freer.

Implying beginning of this sentence is not lost shows signs of ever after.
Extending the ripple seduces while consulting with core current.

Receiving poems nightly trains in pooling time.
By this scriptive biomechanism time spirals out literal.

We have to want to be here even feeling the current to be.
The view is reader's in view from the start.

Even with no one the writing stays.
Enough ripples in the water to sustain a moving thought nearing its music.

I'm trying to understand action in itself knowing itself.
I've asked you here today to help me say in such a way simply hearing.

Hunger for referents is the way I'm addicted.
Merit deserves sounding meretricious turning tricks.

Every breath is not the only word for it.
You may as well say sex as you do.

Is this another bird page the way poem takes time outside itself?
Animal enjoyment of being studied is curious.

The word is allowed to slide off center into self studiously evolving.
We reflect in such a way that the beginning of the present sentence is infused past.

Time sneaks by. Looking out is back. Line piles. Open the window.

Hanging on for dear life is hardwired in.
Trouble with thinking god it's hard to feel the mood.
Catch the inner force or flee is another mode divide.

The secret is inside at the exact point that outside indistinguishes sharpest.
Autonomous writing appears to threaten domesticity but not without nesting.
Why do anything but it knows in doing.

We're so far over the edge the earth is but a ledge.

Values coagulate to cross the great water.
Truth shifts with a shuffle.

Alienation is birth pains healing with fresh distance.
Context serves understanding but its force of approval trivializes.
We have to let these thoughts go on thinking in us.

Losing track of musical drive pervasive in days ends overthinking.
Axial drives straight through by dead-reckoning retention.

Raga takes hold in the long stretch.
Stray religion as against wake the fuck up.

Everything is in training for the present moment and its *big boing* outside.
Poem catches you up in its map feeling guided in this very here.

Goethe Rilke & other ragas rippling back within hearing.
The present can't help seeding past present.

28 *what you see is not what you get*

...only when it's funny...
Roger Rabbit

I'm here to discover how I'm drawn.
People mostly count the things done wrong, am I right?

There's a poetics of dayworker on streetcorner out to get work for the night.
A word a line a poem therefore I am.

Entering an other attentional zone.
Compassionate compression tones.

Realistic presentation endangering the rising real better be good.
If criticism looks to stabilize attitudes good luck in these woods.

No stopping to evaluate but letting in the missing.
The how of arising is evasion.

Why is it time needs to pass before I like what is written?
There are complexities you never can get your life around.

A poem is language able to instruct in its singular dynamic just passing through.
Abandon all scope trope ye who enter here.

The mood of spurious indicative is upon us as follows.
Funny is better.

A line is the site of temporary insanity.
Wherefore the mood that doesn't know its name.

There are moments in the body when you don't know where you are.

Actual time is the one I believe is happening.
Confusion is moving right along.

The temporal concept is under pressure to reverse.
The idea is I'm thinking for you about you too.

There's nothing that doesn't scare something else.
This saying is circling itself—wagons? vultures?
If you're asking it's not the peak.

I visualize my life as my perfected visualization.
There is no pinpoint on despair while love floods.

The split gut shows the mind crack running right through.
Your doing for me but not as me completes me for now.

I scare easy.
Struggle registers in the gut beneath accommodating smiles.

Half standing he's a lie down comic.
The music's a rock in the hand.

Fatigue with difficult text furthers space for the next.
Every Duchampian word a work of art life is.

The actual form is glimpsed in reflection passing.

There are places in the mind where you don't know when you are.

No more small thinking like attaining enlightenment.
I'm cultivating a secret garden as the spot thinking takes refuge on my behalf.

Beyond this I go missing.
I don't pretend there's somewhere to go that isn't already gone.

Waving hello where in our compound we share letters.
Hand held in mind writing.

Nouns don't seem to like me anymore.
This isn't like you, non plus.

One language is like another when it feels like it.
At heart in the sentence is round dance.

Inapparently there's light inside light giving heat species specific.
Hence the hand rubbing showing as we are.

Don't touch me intimately shields the body against literality.
The issue goes back and forth on me like renewing Jerusalem.

The body is not as dumb as it looks.
Stumbles center new.

Poetic kills and cures like food feeds poisoning.
At once or never.

Reading what is written I believe the unbelievable.
Why assign negative meaning to what only means what you assign it?
Meaning the pull is a good rung further down.

Sin's sign of deoptimized being's post right mind.
The real stuff is shall we say *dys*witheld.
Mind stumbles into death's *haha*.

The river of attitudes soon reaches highwater.
"Even the brain knows we're built to speak from the left."
Words smell.

Native tongue knows it's going to hell in a hand task kit.
We're the school with no lunch.
Poem feeds mind while starving and by no means only.

It makes you ill with food gone off while inoculating against the familiar.
Surviving as some poets don't may preserve immune system gains, no guilt.
Language is inherently mind-degradable, just try saying the same over & over.

Charnel birth celebration is at hand as always.
The poem's chaos is the beyond it keeps for you.
The outside sustains a further than.

May the great praying mantis strike the pose of communion with *our* dead.
Confusion refuses with the force of inner fuse.

We know these dimensions by the heat of their leaks.

32 *tone burn*

Prajna is the logic of dharma flashing in mind
painfully rare.
Ontononymous the Particular

I can't say I'm not reading mind at your expense.
The choice to abide at the intersection of dimensions is unstable non-conceivably.
A poem is said to dimension further.

Things the poem is not doing to satisfy you are available elsewhere.
If it depended on approval it would never be.
Revelatory is the fact of meaning.

It fields mind time.
The sense of vehicle includes road feel—just saying *feeler roading reader mode.*
Feeling flashes faster than conceived.

Hereby it specifically avoids my personality to the point of further doubt.
It gives me surrender to the manyness of any one.
Now discover a culinary approach to breath followed by lips glimpsing eros.

Fuck fear. Cook air.
Penetrate to the soft interior atremble.
Dagger moment's when the daimon reaches across to you, ready or not.

It shows a poetry before its readership yet in the illusion of isolation.
It lets me cry out to dislodge memory's commitment to failure.
Why embarrass the world by representing it inevitably badly?

Who knows what *it* is.
Truth sweeps you through. Clear scape.
It tunes attracting being into its view where an ear slips through.

The true line consumes completely leaving nothing.
The string sings for its text.

We may not be able to tell our selves apart but one's own other can.
The world becomes more dangerous the freer you are, then less.

Life is the wait while showing through.
This proves being from nowhere.

Noticing space empty is as it isn't.
The unsayable is what is said between one more and another, plus contrary.

Catching the current knows the change neither inside nor out yet around, going on.
You glove.

On the earth is in the earth, body in body.
Ghost words, ghostlier syntax, we notate around, thereon, wherever.

A line completes when it is nothing.
Empty space proves unborn poetry and non-existing but not non-dancing in itself.

Caring less is less care overall.
Channel fall, thoughtless compassion, charnel all.

Palpate to touch onto seed ideas still torquing all through.
You are what you recognize.
Called forward calls home by the book.

The book ends to face death in every line.
Happy hopelessness is like meditating on not meditating.
I'm pretending to be awake in as much as I am.

Line colors mind as each word verbs, just alleging.
The book in a way of speaking goes home on all threes.
It wants you to learn to read all over so it can talk through you, thrice born.

We're momentarily undistracted by sense-making need.
Why the attachment to this version of reality?
Vile habit with style beguiles.

Manyworldliness frees mind from rightness and its righteousness.
If it's not at least slightly indigestible why say truth?
Birth trusts by unexampled force, naturally.

I am to my body as my body is to earth, intimately.
Breathing weathers, reasoning webs.
Born preverbal, unborn preverbial.

Miming empty space shows its dancing ways.
Wise crazy doesn't look crazy no wise.
The end talks funny to itself to stay hands free.

The big picture doesn't fit in our frames but we can't stop trying.
Still wishing to satisfy our secret basic need for uncertainty.
I hide my split in thirds taking refuge in contraries.
Laying my four in voice on top bottoms in bounds for ends.

pre limn

Poiesis is singularity in motion.

Ontononymous the Particular

pre limn

In the *pre* note to the previous large collection of preverbs, *Not Even Rabbits Go Down This Hole*, I emphasized the work's commitment to performative participation in *linguality*, understood as the unavoidable fact of language creating "reality" as we conceive it. I see poiesis, at least the poiesis I call *axial*, as conscious engagement with what is necessarily an *alternate* linguality. Alternate to the creative force of language in any other manifestation because singular, and therefore different from what came before or is occurring elsewhere. It can go from gently odd to fully alien while *just itself* in the middle. "Difference" or "uniqueness" in this species of work is not something contrived for effect; rather, it's something come upon in the course of unfolding language accessing its resources—happening in the mind or on the page, "same difference." Difference is intrinsic to singularity.[1] And so is the new sameness newly created.

Some notions come along to help us keep a potentially alienating situation safely on the creative end of a spectrum of possible relationships; notions like

> *A poet may live largely in preemptive exile.*
>
> *Language is the literal limen between self and the receding world.*
>
> *Linguality grows in creative diversity where the traffic is two-way.*
>
> *Poiesis intensifies the process of cocreation in the between.*

And all such declarations leave the key options of understanding open. It's a matter of poietic practicality. Openness in meaning leaves room for further life. And it leaves constraint up to the reader. No coercion of correctness in reading.

---

[1] My thought may be related to Wallace Steven's insight—"The essential fault of surrealism is that it invents without discovering"—although I hardly agree with the apparent dismissal of historical Surrealism.

Reading is free to have never been before.

To join in the fray of affectionate Keats abuse, I would call poietic necessity a *willing suspension of belief*—where disbelief is moot. It seems pretty obvious that it's impossible to function at any given moment without belief in something—*no meteor will strike ground between here and the corner*—but the real concern is the consequential long-term beliefs, those that set limits on basic psychonautic behavior; those beliefs that don't come and go like what's good for breakfast.

Blanket belief leaves our alternate minds under the cover.

The persistent beliefs—belief *fields*, really—are layers showing up like tips of icebergs, semi-accessible planes, out-of-sight-out-of-mind networks conducting business behind the back. (An actual "secret state" on the personal plane.) So, poiesis aims to *suspend* in order to *let show*. And that translates to: *no preconditions to the sayable.*

Poiesis = risk.
Axiality = precarity.

Axial poiesis is an instance of *elective self-orientation*—a generative process knowing where it's going—without external guidance—where poet mind (the presumed conductor) is not necessarily directly in the know. Or the guidance, the global reckoning, is active in layers to which one is able to gain access—meaning that the poem going forward is evidence of being *in place on the move, self-knowingly*. It offers revelation about being at rest *here*, however much here is changing or seems to be slipping away.

Self-orientation on the neurophysiological level is *proprioception*—the built-in system of self-orientation through neurological array, operating in our every action-in-relation—how you manage to tie your shoes in the dark. Since Charles Olson's *Proprioception* (1965) this psychomaterial dimension of self-knowing in the world has been present in our consciousness of poetics. David Bohm contrasted the orientational body system with how we do our thinking: *We could say that practically all the problems of the human race are due to the fact that thought is not proprioceptive.* Thinking drives forward without benefit of sharp and immediate *feedback* from its activated field of containment—on a scale that is both intimate and inclusively surrounding.

But what if mind, and therefore thought, and therefore poiesis, has the potential to (re)claim proprioception in its conscious modus operandi? Proprioception is trainable, extendable, transpositional; we can enhance it, perhaps "evolve" it further. As a t'ai chi practitioner I have long been convinced of this potential for *creative* proprioception. I see it possible that not only thinking but language can (re)discover intrinsic capacity for proprioception and its further embodiments.

Axial poiesis emphasizes flexibility of self-orientation in unfolding language. In extension, self-orientation discovers it's not guiding a thing or an enclosed entity but acting as attractor in a resonant field. One has "identity" within the dynamic of the field—with a point of focus in center/periphery oscillation. And the act of (self)identification includes whatever is communicatively interacting within the field—the operative *sense* is *ecoproprioception*—self-awareness afield—registering self as non-separate from a living surround.

Preverbs come into being through such fielding self-awareness operative *within syntax*—and in the most intensely contained expression, a single line. A containment whose energy comes from nurtured and variable diversity.

thoughts retained in self-diverse linguality

There's little left to be said and everything still to say. This is the forever premise of the fact of poetry. It says what could be true were we willing. At the baseline is a willingness to embrace a certain intensity of unknowing. There's consent to follow an implicit possibility of further knowing of an unknown kind. And another given: the intuited promise of a new intensity. Speaking it seems to spring from a primal ambivalence. Or polyvalence. The rough stuff of dreams.

Working within alternative thought frames lets things find their diverse ways. A line is a thought frame within a larger thought frame—poem, then series, then book, with world ever alongside. Frames within frames, embedded, conversing.

Frames are a dime a nano.
[future folk saying]

The work of Blake and Goethe, for instance, valorizes a dynamic complementarity of—a high voltage oscillation between—imagination and rationality. In a further view of that principle, one recognizes a poetics of imagination and rationality separately and together working at an edge of incommensurability—a creative matrix with a certain turbulence. Axial poiesis need not resolve what it engages. Or reconcile its differences.

divorce is a subcategory of marriage
when not the contrary

Nothing gets worked out. It leads (intransitive/transitive) through proprioceiving oscillation.

axial = rising free play at the heart of plumbline gravity

Axial poiesis works toward a retention of energetically focused non-resolution, however perplexing. The poetics here is difficult to describe in a way that doesn't violate its principle. The goal of this sense of poetics is not mainly understanding, rather it aims for further engagement with intent to reveal. Mind process in axial language *enters into meaning by entrainment.*

para-duality

I find it helpful at this moment to declare a principle of *para-duality.* Whereas "non-duality" intends an essential non-separateness of contraries, para-duality pairs non-separateness and a *retained separateness*—grounds for further distinction.

Something is always left hanging by the thought until read.
Ontononymous the Particular

At the peak of embrace or experienced "oneness" in poiesis there remains a shadow otherness. This residuality incites the unfelt. Things/beings remember their actual singularity; at the same time, this *implicate singularity* retains consciousness of non-separateness from otherness. Difference is not exclusive of non-difference. Middles have never liked being excluded.

Axial poiesis hits the road without its reading skills. It practices non-dexterity with an accuracy that starts with (re)balancing, 100% on the spot. A preverb enables thinking language to find its balance mid-stride by the nano.

Wobble discovers its counter-wobble and the pivot liberates.

(Verbs can be transitive and intransitive at once, not to mention reflexive, so to speak jussively.)

Axial poiesis is on alert for lingual spaces with little thought already settled inside, a sheer absence that allows the unthought to show up amidst our emergently vivid lacks. I sometimes sense writing is a search for my missing genes. It teaches me I'm the kind of poet who was born (not made) without a full deck to play with. It was clear I had to invent my own game. This means giving up aspirations for a firm fit.

poiesis
requires unmaking
like the love bed
you get way out in

the continuum of axial poiesis runs from exile's sadness to hilaritas sublime

Axial poiesis is language on the alert for further self-evidence. Happening right before your eyes and far in your ears at once. Axial *reading* is the space of its own discovery/recovery—and its *emergent self-evidence*. Its instance suggests justification is inappropriate behavior.

The axial principle knows it has never not been. It's self-evident as long as there's *now* awake to itself. Of course that doesn't necessarily mean we actually recognize it as such.

Poiesis expresses as well psyche's intention to mate with its inner other gender. This is a pairing longing to see itself in action. Self-diverse. It requires a lot of unobstructed mind space just to get started. And once it gets moving it refuses to exploit its own momentum. It returns to zero point, for "good measure," the refreshing gap in pattern.

Poet is reborn in the thought *This doesn't fit known categories and now has to be said.*

One can fail to achieve a complete statement and yet induce further knowing.

Accordingly a preverb happens in search of a writer-reader to perform completion, a singularity with no apparent connection to the poet as source.

No need to think nothing before thinking anything and nothing but.
Ontononymous

If it could be said more clearly I'd say count me in, but I don't dream of such a thing. Not anymore. There are better ways to not succeed while linguality moves on.

A failure exposes an imposed burden of credibility.

Authority counts on being irresistible. And in the field of its motion authority tends to deactivate what it controls. Axial poiesis does not remain in one place long enough to give authority a clear shot. One thing you can count on is that authority never stops aiming, while authorship sails in variable waters.

Any actualized space of activated vision attracts more of the same—stepped up intensity of realized singularity.

axial disclaimer

No other poetics has been invalidated in the making of this text.

And no other poetics is fully embraced; in fact, even its own poetics, at a given stage of realization, is not invariably embraced beyond its moment. Nevertheless it operates beyond basic doubt; it takes necessary action as absolute necessity.

post-claimer

There's a kind of isolation in one's truest work. It runs parallel to a certain gratitude in discovering a work's action according to core principle. This would seem to mean that reception is positive or that a reader "understands" the work; but that's not it. Positive response is undeniably satisfying, likewise accounts of understanding (whatever it actually means to a given reader). Yet what is vitally important is that some readers enter the actual state of the work. It's as though the work itself seeks a certain satisfaction in readerly continuance, and may even register the probability of such eventuality. And in a work's continuance it seems to sense when it's getting through. And where it gets through to.

Acknowledgements & Admissions

Poet mind is easily confused by abstractions like *wide readership, reputation, place in history, critical acclaim,* etc. Duchamp said it's not the artist's business—history decides. From time to time it's worth (re)affirming actual values beyond these most ephemeral, imprecise, and largely inapplicable (or at least undecidable) concerns—those for which there's never an end in sight. Of course our species sociability, not to mention inevitable but no less strange exposure to fame adoration, urges us from an early age to seek the kind of success these notions seem to promote; and it's nearly impossible to shake it all off. But once a poet discovers the feel of *one's own path*—the flow of its own accord—such notions may seem rather empty; and they can be highly distracting and gravely counter-inspirational.

And there's the ancient notion, which some of our most revered predecessors embodied a version of, that poetry is not first of all, or mainly, a career, but something at root closer to an inescapable vision leading to a life work, even a mission, perhaps even an obsession, indeed a hazardous commitment. Famously Rilke advised a young poet to avoid it if at all possible. Such a view today might seem to some an empty sentimental posturing, but most of us know certain of those who indeed paid the price.

It has long been clear to me that I don't want my work to burden the mind but to attract it to its further capacity. I'm not a good Dadaist. My *icons* find their *clasts* closer to home, and when confronted they sometimes turn around and smile with wily repentance, only to strike out with renewed force as the focus shifts. And the work seems to have high AQ (alienation quotient). It requires an elusive native alignment to find a fit worth encouraging. Forced fit—the coercive hold of authority—nails even imaginal feet to the floor. Coercion is the true enemy of art as of life. Poiesis is for the willing mind. And willingness is self-selecting and -regulating.

That said (at too great length), I feel only gratitude for the actual reading that happens in the work's own register. My idiopathic mysticism includes the sense that work thrives on energic feedback from such aligned reading, even unconsciously; nevertheless, there are joys in finding out about it. I'm grateful indeed to the editors who have published this work[1] or recorded it as publication[2] and those who have taken the time to address it in writing.[3] It reminds me that poiesis is deeply collaborative with the possible reader. In my many years of collaboration with Charles Stein we have often acknowledged that even a single true reader can sustain one's work. And ongoing collaboration with Susan Quasha is proof restorative. With that focus one can experience a bounty beyond the calculable. And the work finds its further play right where it happens—at zero point.

Barrytown, New York
July 2021

---

[1] Poems 12 and 13 from *Flayed Flaws & Other Finagled Opacities* appeared in *Marsh Hawk Review* (Fall 2017), ed. Thomas Fink. *Polypoikilos: Matrix In Variance* was published as a virtual chapbook on *Dispatches from the Poetry Wars* (August 9, 2017: www.dispatchespoetrywars.com), ed. Michael Boughn and Kent Johnson.

[2] Christopher Funkhouser over the past few years has been recording my reading through all the volumes of preverbs, so far having posted over twenty hours now available on PennSound, including poems from this book (writing.upenn.edu/pennsound/x/Quasha.php). See note 3 below for Funkhouser's essay on the process and experience or recording.

[3] I'm indebted to Burt Kimmelman for both his writing about my work and his editing of the collection of sixteen essays, *Zero Point Poiesis: George Quasha's Axial Art*, foreword by Jerome McGann and essays by, respectively, Carter Ratcliff, Gary Shapiro, Cheryl Pallant, Edward Casey, Robert Kelly, Kimberly Lyons, Burt Kimmelman, William Benton, Andrew Joron, Charles Stein, Matt Hill, Tamas Panitz, Christopher Funkhouser, and Vyt Bakaitis (Aporeia, 2022).

Contents by Poem Title

Tuning by Fire *9*

Rippling Scales *81*

Waking from Myself *153*

Mirroring by Alterity *225*

Single Poem Dedications

Page 234: *red is for knowing ahead still unprepared* is for Sherry Williams on the occasion of her exhibition in Catskill (9-16-17)

Page 235: "*mirroring by alterity*" is for Robert Kelly on his birthday (9-24-17)

About the Author

George Quasha is a poet, artist, musician and writer working in diverse mediums to explore certain principles (e.g., *axiality, ecoproprioception*). For his primary medium poiesis he has invented the genre *preverbs* as a medium of axial language and "linguality at zero point." Seven of the thirteen books of *preverbs* have been published to date. *Poetry in Principle: Essays in Poetics* (foreword by Edward Casey, 2019) contains recent writing on "the poetics of thinking."

Zero Point Poiesis: George Quasha's Axial Art (2022) is a collection of writings on his poetry, art and thought by sixteen authors, edited by Burt Kimmelman, foreword by Jerome McGann.

He has been awarded the T-Space 10th annual Poetry Award (2022).

His ongoing video work was awarded a Guggenheim Fellowship (2006), principally for *art is/music is/poetry is (Speaking Portraits)*, for which he has recorded over a thousand artists, poets, and composers in eleven countries saying what art, music, or poetry *is* (art-is-international.org)—represented in the book *art is (Speaking Portraits)* (2016).

His axial stones, drawings and video have been exhibited in various venues, including the Snite Museum of Art, the Manfred Baumgartner Gallery, White Box, the Samuel Dorsky Museum and biennials (Poland, Switzerland, New York).

Axial Stones: An Art of Precarious Balance (foreword by Carter Ratcliff, 2006) explores the axial principle in his sculpture. Other writing on art includes *An Art of Limina: Gary Hill's Works & Writings* (with Charles Stein, foreword by Lynne Cooke, 2009).

Books of poetry previous to *preverbs* include *Somapoetics* (1973), *Giving the Lily Back Her Hands* (1979), and *Ainu Dreams* (with Chie Hasegawa [Hammons], 1999).

Edited anthologies include *America a Prophecy: A New Reading of American Poetry from Pre-Colombian Times to the Present* (with Jerome Rothenberg, 1973/2012), *Open Poetry: Four Anthologies of Expanded Poems* (with Ronald Gross, plus Emmett Williams, John Robert Colombo, & Walter Lowenfels, 1973), *An Active Anthology* (with Susan Quasha, 1974), and *The Station Hill Blanchot Reader* (with Charles Stein, 1999).

He lives in Barrytown, New York, collaborating with Susan Quasha on photography/preverbs (six series of their sixteen combined works available online), and together they publish Station Hill Press.